Lebanese Cookbook

Enjoy Authentic Lebanese Cooking with Easy Lebanese Recipes

By
BookSumo Press
All rights reserved

Published by
http://www.booksumo.com

ENJOY THE RECIPES?
KEEP ON COOKING WITH 6 MORE FREE COOKBOOKS!

Visit our website and simply enter your email address to join the club and receive your 6 cookbooks.

http://booksumo.com/magnet

https://www.instagram.com/booksumopress/

https://www.facebook.com/booksumo/

LEGAL NOTES

All Rights Reserved. No Part Of This Book May Be Reproduced Or Transmitted In Any Form Or By Any Means. Photocopying, Posting Online, And / Or Digital Copying Is Strictly Prohibited Unless Written Permission Is Granted By The Book's Publishing Company. Limited Use Of The Book's Text Is Permitted For Use In Reviews Written For The Public.

Table of Contents

Roasted Bell Hummus 9

Classic Tabbouli Salad 10

Black Lebanese Pilaf 11

Zesty Hummus 12

Spring Bulgur 13

Lebanese Chicken Kabobs 14

Classic Arabian Lentils Soup 15

Semolina Diamonds with Lemon Syrup 16

Golden Lebanese Potato Salad 17

Lebanese Potato and Lentils Soup 18

Cinnamon Chicken Kabobs 19

Creamy Garlic Aioli 20

Grilled Chicken with Yogurt Sauce 21

Lebanese Potato Sauce 22

Saucy Lamb Casserole 23

Alien Edamame Hummus 24

Feta and Eggplant Bake 25

Honey Chicken with Couscous 26

Lebanese Real Spice 27

Classic Lebanese Rice and Lentils Pilaf 28

Traditional Lebanese Bread 29

Lentil Feta Salad 30

Chickpea Falafels 31

Homemade Lebanese Pita Bread 32

Spicy Bread 33

Crispy Sumac Eggs 34

Mediterranean Spicy Shawarma 35

Spicy Chicken and Nutty Rice Skillet 36

Spicy Beef and Spinach Rice Stew 37

Broken Hearts Salad 38

Red Bean Salad 39

Navy Beans Soup 40

Lebanese Meatloaf Rolls 41

Lemon Lentils Soup 42

Nutty Lebanese Kebaa 43

Homemade Oregano Pizza 44

Summer Hearts Soup 45

Golden Roasted Chicken 46

Sumac Spring Salad 47

Classic Minty Lebanese Tabbouli 48

Homemade Flat Lebanese Bread 49

Rosy Almonds Pudding 50

Nutty Short Cookies 51

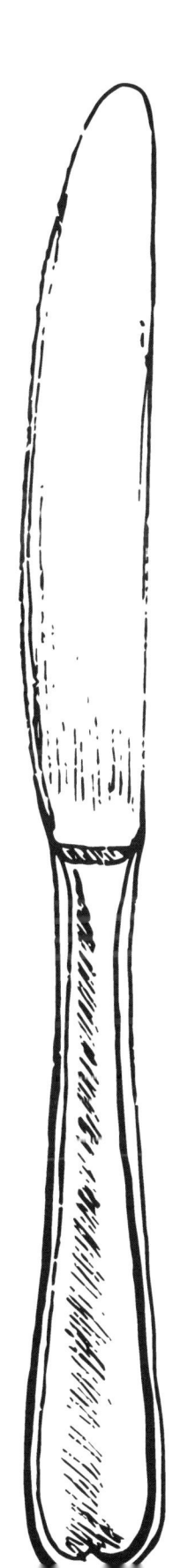

Golden Rice and Raisins Pudding 52

Shawarma Pie 53

Crispy Zucchini Salad 54

Hummus Boats 55

Beef Loaf with Yogurt 56

Sumac Bread 57

Summer Lentils Pilaf 58

Creamy Steak Baguettes 59

Midnight Lemon Salad 60

Roasted Lemon Potato Casserole 61

Vermicelli Rice 62

Crunchy Tomato and Cabbage Salad 63

Blushing Tuna Salad 64

Creamy Black Salad 65

Nutty Lamb Pierogis 66

Golden Cauliflower Bites with Tahini 68

Spicy Beef and Squash Skillet 69

Golden Chickpeas 70

Lemon Wings 71

Yogurt and Chickpea Bake 72

Sweet and Salty Lovers Skillet 73

Nutty Lamb Rolls 74

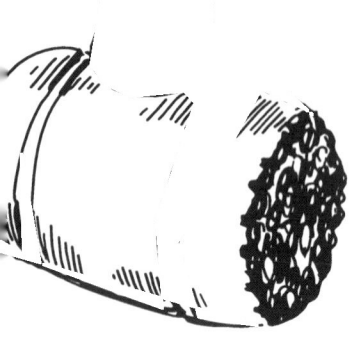

Crunchy Beet Salad 75

Spicy Chicken Roast 76

Spring Veggies Salad with Tahini Sauce 77

Fruity Carrot Salad 78

Beef Kufta Casserole 79

Arabian Tomato Sauce 80

Pomegranate Flowers Salad 81

Classic Lebanese Chicken Kabobs 82

Homemade Lebanese Chicken Burritos 83

Minty Warm Mushroom Salad 84

Pistachios Baklava with Honey and Pomegranate Syrup 85

Trick or Treat Date Cookies 87

Saucy Okra Burger Pan 88

Tahini Meatloaf 89

Neon Pilaf 91

Fried Meaty Eggplant Stew 92

Ricy Meatballs Soup 93

Creamy Serrano and Cucumber Salad 94

Lebanese Style Chicken Couscous 95

Tripoli Lamb Gyros 96

Beirut Bread 97

Minty Potato Salad 98

Hot Pepper Hummus Dip 99

Saucy Lamb Stuffed Zucchini 100

Homemade Tahini Hummus 101

Tropical Coconut Cookies 102

Cream Stuffed Potato Boats 103

Creamy Herbed Lentils Salad 104

Classic Dark Baba Ganouj 105

Loulou's Za'atar 106

Za'atar II 107

Alternative Za'atar 108

Roasted Bell Hummus

Prep Time: 20 mins
Total Time: 20 mins

Servings per Recipe: 8
Calories   109.4
Fat   4.0g
Cholesterol   8.3mg
Sodium   533.0mg
Carbohydrates   14.3g
Protein   4.6g

Ingredients

- 1 (15 oz.) cans garbanzo beans, drained
- 1 (4 oz.) jars roasted red peppers
- 3 tbsp lemon juice
- 1 1/2 tbsp tahini
- 1 clove garlic, minced
- 1/2 tsp ground cumin
- 1/2 tsp cayenne pepper
- 1/4 tsp salt
- 1 tbsp chopped parsley
- 1/2 C. crumbled feta cheese

Directions

1. Get a food processor: Place in it the chickpeas, red peppers, Feta, lemon juice, tahini, garlic, cumin, cayenne, and salt.
2. Blend them smooth. Pour the mixture into a serving bowl. Place it in the fridge for 60 min.
3. Garnish your hummus with some parsley then serve it.
4. Enjoy.

CLASSIC
Tabbouli Salad

Prep Time: 30 mins
Total Time: 30 mins

Servings per Recipe: 8
Calories	165.2
Fat	9.0g
Cholesterol	0.0mg
Sodium	57.4mg
Carbohydrates	20.0g
Protein	3.7g

Ingredients

- 5.5 oz. Italian parsley, chopped.
- 6 spring onions, chopped
- 4 large tomatoes, chopped
- 3 lemons, juice
- 5 tbsp olive oil
- 1 C. bulgur
- 1 C. water, boiled
- 1/8 tsp ground black pepper
- 1/8 tsp salt

Directions

1. Get a mixing bowl: Stir in the boiling water with 1 C. of bulgur. Cover it with a kitchen towel. Let it sit until it cools down.
2. Get a large mixing bowl: Toss in it the tomato with onion, parsley, lemon juice, olive oil, and a pinch of salt to make the salad.
3. Add the bulgur to salad and mix them well.
4. Serve your salad with your favorite toppings.
5. Enjoy.

Black Lebanese Pilaf

Prep Time: 25 mins
Total Time: 55 mins

Servings per Recipe: 4
Calories   451.0
Fat   14.7g
Cholesterol   0.0mg
Sodium   16.7mg
Carbohydrates   67.0g
Protein   14.5g

Ingredients

- 4 tbsp olive oil
- 1 medium onion, chopped
- 3 garlic cloves, minced
- 2 tsp ground cumin
- 3/4 tsp ground cinnamon
- 1/2 tsp ground allspice
- 2 (14 oz.) cans vegetable broth
- 3/4 C. dried lentils, rinsed
- 3/4 C. long-grain white rice
- 2 large onions, sliced
- 3 tomatoes, quartered lengthwise
- 1 cucumber, peeled, cut into rounds
- plain yogurt
- chopped mint

Directions

1. Place a large saucepan over medium heat. Heat in it 2 tbsp of olive oil.
2. Add the onion with garlic, cinnamon, allspice, and cumin. Cook them for 5 min.
3. Stir in the lentils with broth. Cook them until they start boiling. Put on the lid and let them cook for 12 min over low heat.
4. Once the time is up, add the rice. Cook them over medium heat until they start boiling
5. Put on the lid and let them cook for 16 min over low medium heat.
6. Place a large pan over medium heat. Heat in it 2 tbsp of oil. Cook in it the onion for 22 min.
7. Adjust the seasoning of the rice pilaf and place it in serving plates.
8. Top it with the caramelized onion. Garnish it with some cucumber, tomato and yogurt. Serve it right away.
9. Enjoy.

ZESTY
Hummus

Prep Time: 5 mins
Total Time: 5 mins

Servings per Recipe: 12
Calories　　　　73.2
Fat　　　　　　3.1g
Cholesterol　　　0.0mg
Sodium　　　　111.8mg
Carbohydrates　 9.4g
Protein　　　　 2.6g

Ingredients

1 (15 oz.) cans chickpeas
1/4 C. tahini paste
3 tbsp lemon juice
1 garlic clove
1/4 tsp ground cumin

salt and pepper

Directions

1. Remove the beans from the water and place it aside. Reserve the water.
2. Get a blender: Place in it all the ingredients. Blend them smooth.
3. Add some of the reserved water to the blender if the mixture is too thick. Serve your hummus as a topping, dip or spread.
4. Enjoy.

Spring Bulgur

Prep Time: 50 mins
Total Time: 50 mins

Servings per Recipe: 4	
Calories	320.3
Fat	18.6g
Cholesterol	0.0mg
Sodium	43.0mg
Carbohydrates	36.6g
Protein	5.3g

Ingredients

- 1/3 C. olive oil
- 1 onion, chopped
- 2 garlic cloves, minced
- 1 tsp dried basil
- 1 C. bulgur
- 1 C. tomatoes, seeded and chopped
- 1 1/2 C. Vegetable broth
- 1 tbsp honey
- 1 tbsp tomato
- salt and pepper
- 1 pinch cayenne
- 2 tbsp chopped parsley

Directions

1. Place a large saucepan over medium heat. Heat in it the oil.
2. Sauté in it the onion for 4 min. Mix in the garlic and cook them for 2 min.
3. Add the basil with tomato and cook them for 3 min. Add the bulgar and mix them well.
4. Stir in the broth and put on the lid. Lower the heat and let them cook for 6 min.
5. Stir in the honey, tomato paste, salt, pepper and cayenne pepper. Let them cook uncovered for 26 min.
6. Once the time is up, turn off the heat and put on the lid. Let it cook for 12 min.
7. Serve your bulgur warm with your favorite toppings.
8. Enjoy.

LEBANESE
Chicken Kabobs

Prep Time: 20 mins
Total Time: 35 mins

Servings per Recipe: 6
Calories   271.5
Fat   13.7g
Cholesterol   80.8mg
Sodium   770.4mg
Carbohydrates   9.4g
Protein   28.0g

Ingredients

6 boneless skinless chicken breasts, diced
3 garlic cloves, crushed
1/4 C. olive oil
1 lemon, juice
1 tbsp paprika
1 (6 oz.) cans tomato paste

1 C. yogurt
2 tbsp sumaq
1 tsp salt
2 tsp black pepper

Directions

1. Before you do anything, preheat the oven grill and grease it.
2. Get a mixing bowl: Whisk in it the garlic with olive oil, lemon juice, paprika, tomato paste, yogurt, sumaq, salt and pepper.
3. Stir the chicken dices into the mixture. Cover it with a plastic wrap and place it in the fridge for at least 1 h.
4. Grease some skewers then thread into them the chicken dices. Place them on the grill and cook them for 4 to 6 min on each side.
5. Serve your chicken kabobs warm with some pita bread and yogurt.
6. Enjoy.

Classic Arabian Lentils Soup

Prep Time: 10 mins
Total Time: 45 mins

Servings per Recipe: 6
Calories   173.4
Fat   1.1g
Cholesterol   0.0mg
Sodium   14.1mg
Carbohydrates   30.0g
Protein   12.2g

Ingredients

- 8 C. water
- 1 1/2 C. small red lentils, rinsed
- 3 Maggi chicken cubes
- 1/2 C. finely diced onion
- 1 garlic clove
- 1 1/2 tsp fresh parsley
- 3/4 tsp cumin
- 1/2-1 tsp turmeric

Directions

1. Place a large pot over medium heat. Stir in it all the ingredients.
2. Cook it until it starts boiling. Put on the lid and let it cook for 36 min over low heat.
3. Once the time is up, serve your soup hot with some lime wedges.
4. Enjoy.

SEMOLINA Diamonds with Lemon Syrup

🥣 Prep Time: 15 mins
🕐 Total Time: 1 hr

Servings per Recipe: 12
Calories 606.9
Fat 15.7g
Cholesterol 33.1mg
Sodium 272.1mg
Carbohydrates 111.7g
Protein 7.4g

Ingredients

CAKE
3 C. semolina
3/4 C. unsweetened butter, melted
3/4 C. sugar
1 1/2 tsp baking soda
1 C. plain yogurt
1/2 C. whole blanched almonds

SYRUP
4 C. sugar
3 C. water
1/2 small lemon, juice

Directions

1. Before you do anything, preheat the oven to 400 F. Grease a 9 inches baking pan. Get a mixing bowl: Combine in it the semolina, sugar and the butter well.
2. Get a small mixing bowl: Whisk in it the soda with yogurt. Let it sit for few minutes until it rise.
3. add it to the semolina bowl and combine them well with your hands. Press the mixture into the greased pan.
4. Use a sharp knife or pizza cutter to cut it into diamonds shapes or squares. Top each semolina diamond with an almond.
5. Place the pan in the oven and cook them for 32 to 46 min.
6. Place a heavy saucepan over medium heat. Whisk in it all the ingredients. Cook them over high heat until they start boiling.
7. Lower the heat and let the syrup cook for an extra 46 min to 60 min until it become slightly thick and coats a metal spoon.
8. Allow the syrup to cool down completely. Pour it over the semolina cake pan while it is hot. Allow it to cool down completely.
9. Serve your semolina diamonds with some tea. Enjoy.

Golden Lebanese Potato Salad

Prep Time: 10 mins
Total Time: 28 mins

Servings per Recipe:	2
Calories	432.6
Fat	20.6 g
Cholesterol	0.0 mg
Sodium	22.1 mg
Carbohydrates	57.5 g
Protein	6.7 g

Ingredients

- canola oil
- 3 potatoes, peeled and cubed
- 2 tbsp cooking onions, chopped
- 1 tsp garlic, minced
- 1 shake cayenne pepper
- 1/2 C. cilantro, chopped
- 1/8-1/4 tsp ground coriander
- ground black pepper
- sea salt
- 3 tbsp olive oil
- 1/2 tsp lime juice

Directions

1. Place a large pan over medium heat. Heat in a splash of canola oil.
2. Add to it the potato and cook them for 8 to 10 min while stirring them often. Drain it and place it aside.
3. Heat the olive oil in the same pan. Sauté in it the onion, minced garlic, cayenne, ground coriander and finely chopped cilantro.
4. Cook them for 2 min. Stir in the cooked potato and toss them to coat. Serve your potato salad warm with your favorite toppings.
5. Enjoy.

LEBANESE POTATO
and Lentils Soup

🍲 Prep Time: 10 mins
🕐 Total Time: 1 hr 40 mins

Servings per Recipe: 8
Calories   144.3
Fat   0.6g
Cholesterol   0.0mg
Sodium   774.7mg
Carbohydrates   28.6g
Protein   8.4g

Ingredients

1 bunch cilantro, stems removed
12 cloves garlic
olive oil
2 1/2 tsp salt, divided
2 large onions, chopped
1 lb. lentils, washed and drained
1 1/2 tsp cinnamon

12 C. water
1 (10 oz.) boxes frozen spinach
2 medium potatoes, cubed
6 tbsp lemon juice

Directions

1. Get a blender: Place in it the cilantro with garlic, 3 Tbsps. olive oil, and 1/2 tsp of salt. Process them until they become smooth.
2. Place a large saucepan over medium heat. Heat in it 1/4 C. of olive oil. Cook in it the onion for 4 min.
3. Stir in the lentils and cook them for an extra 2 min. Stir in the water with cinnamon.
4. Let them cook for 46 min while stirring it every once in a while.
5. Stir in the remaining salt, spinach, potatoes and cilantro mixture. Let the soup cook for an extra 14 min.
6. Stir in the lemon juice and cook them for 12 min over low heat. Adjust the seasoning of the soup then serve it warm.
7. Enjoy.

Cinnamon Chicken Kabobs

Prep Time: 40 mins
Total Time: 50 mins

Servings per Recipe: 4
Calories   259.6
Fat   17.3g
Cholesterol   72.6mg
Sodium   508.0mg
Carbohydrates   1.3g
Protein   23.7g

Ingredients

- 1 lb. chicken breast, cubes
- 1 garlic clove, peeled and crushed
- 3/4 tsp salt
- 1/4 tsp cinnamon
- 1/4 tsp black pepper
- 1/4 tsp allspice
- 2 tbsp olive oil
- 3 tbsp lemon juice

Directions

1. Before you do anything, preheat the grill and grease it.
2. Get a mixing bowl: Mix in it all the ingredients. Cover the bowl with a plastic wrap and place it in the fridge for at least 1 h.
3. Drain the chicken pieces from the marinade and thread them into skewers.
4. Place the chicken kabobs on the grill and cook them for 4 to 6 min on each side.
5. Serve your chicken kabobs with your favorite toppings.
6. Enjoy.

CREAMY
Garlic Aioli

🥣 Prep Time: 5 mins
🕐 Total Time: 5 mins

Servings per Recipe: 14
Calories   425.6
Fat   46.7g
Cholesterol   0.0mg
Sodium   174.8mg
Carbohydrates   2.6g
Protein   0.8g

Ingredients

- 3 C. corn oil
- 1 C. lemon juice
- 1 head garlic
- 2 egg whites
- 1 tsp salt

Directions

1. Get a food processor: Place in it all the ingredients. Blend them smooth.
2. Place the aioli in the fridge for at least 1 h then serve it.
3. Enjoy.

Grilled Chicken with Yogurt Sauce

Prep Time: 15 mins
Total Time: 35 mins

Servings per Recipe: 4
Calories	284.4
Fat	7.0g
Cholesterol	149.6mg
Sodium	569.6mg
Carbohydrates	2.9g
Protein	49.5g

Ingredients

1/2 C. plain yogurt
2 tsp lemon zest
2 tbsp lemon juice
1 garlic clove, crushed
1/2 tsp ground cumin
1/2 tsp ground coriander
1/2 tsp red pepper flakes
1/2 tsp black pepper
1/2 tsp salt
2 lbs. boneless skinless chicken

Directions

1. Get a mixing bowl: Whisk in it the yogurt with lemon zest, lemon juice, garlic, cumin, coriander, pepper flakes, black pepper and salt.
2. Coat the chicken pieces with the yogurt sauce. Place the chicken pieces in the fridge for at least 30 min.
3. Before you do anything, preheat the grill and grease it.
4. Place the chicken pieces over the grill and cook them for 8 to 12 min on each side.
5. Serve your grilled chicken with your favorite toppings.
6. Enjoy.

LEBANESE
Potato Sauce

🥘 Prep Time: 10 mins
🕐 Total Time: 25 mins

Servings per Recipe: 10
Calories   146.3
Fat   11.0g
Cholesterol   0.0mg
Sodium   352.9mg
Carbohydrates   11.4g
Protein   1.4g

Ingredients

3 small russet potatoes, peeled
1 head garlic
1/3 C. lemon juice

1/2 tbsp salt
1/2 C. canola oil

Directions

1. Place a large pot of water over medium heat. Bring it to a boil. Add the potatoes and cook them until they become soft.
2. Peel the garlic and roughly chop it.
3. Get a food processor: Combine in it the garlic with lemon juice, oil and salt. Process them until they become smooth.
4. Add the mashed potato to the mixture gradually while blending them all the time.
5. Place the sauce in the fridge until it cools down completely then serve it.
6. Enjoy.

Saucy Lamb Casserole

Prep Time: 45 mins
Total Time: 1 hr 45 mins

Servings per Recipe: 6
Calories   305.1
Fat   22.0g
Cholesterol   65.4mg
Sodium   1250.1mg
Carbohydrates   13.2g
Protein   14.9g

Ingredients

1 large eggplant, sliced and unpeeled
1 lb. ground lamb
1 (22 oz.) cans chopped tomatoes
1/2 tsp cinnamon
1 tbsp salt
pepper

1/4 tsp clove
2 crushed garlic cloves
2 medium onions, sliced
2 - 3 tbsp melted butter

Directions

1. Before you do anything, preheat the oven to 450 F. Grease a casserole dish with the melted butter.
2. Place the eggplant slices in a deep dish. Sprinkle over it some salt and let it rest for 32 min.
3. Remove the eggplants and discard the water.
4. Place a large skillet over medium heat. Cook in it the meat with onion for 8 min.
5. Stir in the garlic and cook them for 2 min. Discard the fat.
6. Place a large saucepan over medium heat. Mix in it the tomato with cinnamon, clove, and a salt. Heat them for 3 min.
7. Spread half of the meat mixture in the bottom of the casserole then top it with half of the eggplant slices and half of the tomato mixture.
8. Repeat the process to make another layer. Place a piece of foil over the casserole to cover it.
9. Place the casserole in the oven and cook it for 60 min. Serve it hot with some rice.
10. Enjoy.

ALIEN Edamame Hummus

Prep Time: 10 mins
Total Time: 10 mins

Servings per Recipe: 3
Calories	641.2
Fat	43.2g
Cholesterol	0.0mg
Sodium	1968.4mg
Carbohydrates	47.4g
Protein	23.4g

Ingredients

- 3/4 C. boiled edamame, shells removed
- 1 C. frozen chopped spinach
- 1 (12 oz.) cans garbanzo beans, drained
- 6 garlic cloves
- 1/2 C. tahini
- 1/4-1/2 C. olive oil
- 2 tsp sea salt
- 1 tbsp red pepper flakes

Directions

1. Get a blender: Place in it all the ingredients. Blend them smooth.
2. Serve your hummus with some veggies, pita bread, or toss some of it with a salad.
3. Enjoy.

Feta and Eggplant Bake

🥣 Prep Time: 20 mins
🕐 Total Time: 1 hr

Servings per Recipe: 6
Calories   143.4
Fat   7.0g
Cholesterol   110.8mg
Sodium   628.3mg
Carbohydrates   13.8g
Protein   8.0g

Ingredients

1 large eggplant, peeled and sliced
cooking spray
1 (15 oz.) cans stewed tomatoes
4 oz. feta cheese, crumbled
1/2 C. parsley, minced
1/4 C. cilantro, minced
3 large eggs, beaten
1 large onion, chopped

1/2 tsp salt
1/4 tsp black pepper
1/4 tsp ground allspice
1/4 tsp dry oregano
1/4 tsp ground sage
1 pinch cayenne

Directions

1. Before you do anything, preheat the oven to 300 F. Grease a baking dish.
2. Place a large skillet over medium heat. Grease it with some oil.
3. Place in it the eggplant slices and let them cook for 4 to 5 min on each side.
4. Drain the eggplant slices and lay them in the bottom of the baking dish. Top it with the stewed tomato, feta, parsley, and cilantro.
5. Get a mixing bowl: Mix in it the eggs, onion, salt, pepper, allspice, oregano, sage and cayenne.
6. Spread the mixture all over the tomato layer. Cover it loosely with a piece of foil.
7. Place the casserole in the oven and let it cook for 32 min. Discard the cover and let it cook for an extra 16 to 20 min.
8. Serve your eggplant casserole warm.
9. Enjoy.

HONEY CHICKEN
with Couscous

🍳 Prep Time: 15 mins
🕐 Total Time: 45 mins

Servings per Recipe: 4
Calories   371.9
Fat   4.7g
Cholesterol   76.0mg
Sodium   248.1mg
Carbohydrates   47.3g
Protein   33.2g

Ingredients

4 boneless skinless chicken breasts
1/3 C. onion, chopped
1 clove garlic, minced
1 tbsp butter
2 tsp orange zest
1/2 C. orange juice
1/4 tsp salt

1/4 tsp cinnamon
1/8 tsp allspice
2 tbsp honey
1 C. couscous

Directions

1. Place a large pan over medium heat. Melt in it the butter.
2. Add the chicken, onion and garlic. Cook them for 7 min while stirring them often.
3. Stir in the orange zest, orange juice and salt. Cook them until they start boiling.
4. Lower the heat and put on the lid. Let them cook for an extra 6 min.
5. Stir in the cinnamon with honey and allspice. Let the chicken cook for an extra 6 min uncovered.
6. Prepare the couscous by following the instructions on the package.
7. Serve your honey chicken with couscous.
8. Enjoy.

Lebanese Real Spice

Prep Time: 10 mins
Total Time: 10 mins

Servings per Recipe: 1
Calories   370.6
Fat   17.7g
Cholesterol   0.0mg
Sodium   89.1mg
Carbohydrates   63.4g
Protein   12.9g

Ingredients

- 1/2 C. whole black peppercorn
- 1/4 C. whole coriander seed
- 1/4 C. cassia
- 1/4 C. whole cloves
- 1/3 C. cumin seed
- 2 tsp whole cardamom seeds
- 4 whole nutmegs
- 1/2 C. ground paprika

Directions

1. Grate the nutmeg and place it aside.
2. Get a spice grinder or a blender. Combine in it the remaining ingredients. Process them until they become powdered.
3. Pour the mixture into a mason jar and seal it. Use your spice mixture whenever you desire.
4. Enjoy.

CLASSIC
Lebanese Rice and Lentils Pilaf

🥣 Prep Time: 2 mins
🕒 Total Time: 1 hr 2 mins

Servings per Recipe: 8
Calories   150.6
Fat   3.3g
Cholesterol   0.0mg
Sodium   6.2mg
Carbohydrates   26.1g
Protein   4.4g

Ingredients

1 C. lentils
1 C. brown rice
4 -5 small onions, sliced
1 1/2 tbsp olive oil
3 -4 C. water
2 tbsp lemon juice
Garlic, chopped

1/4 tsp cumin
1/4 tsp pepper
1/4 tsp cayenne
1/2 tsp salt

Directions

1. Place a pot over medium heat. Heat in it the oil. Add the lentils and cook them for 3 min.
2. Stir in the 3 C. of water and cook them until they start boiling. Let it cook for 14 to 16 min.
3. Place a large pan over medium heat. Heat in it a splash of oil. Cook in it the onion with garlic for 3 min.
4. Stir in the rice and cook them for an extra 2 min. Add the lemon juice with a pinch of cumin, cayenne pepper, black pepper and salt.
5. Stir the mixture into the lentils. Cook them until it starts simmering.
6. Lower the heat and put on half a lid. Let it cook for 42 to 46 min while stirring it from time to time.
7. Once the time is up, fluff the pilaf with a fork then serve it warm.
8. Enjoy.

Traditional Lebanese Bread

Prep Time: 30 mins
Total Time: 50 mins

Servings per Recipe:	12
Calories	231.6
Fat	4.8g
Cholesterol	26.2mg
Sodium	334.1mg
Carbohydrates	40.5g
Protein	5.8g

Ingredients

- 1 (1/4 oz.) package active dry yeast
- 1 C. warm water
- 1/4 C. white sugar
- 3 tbsp milk
- 1 egg, beaten
- 1 1/2 tsp salt
- 4 1/2 C. bread flour
- 2 tsp minced garlic
- 1/4 C. melted butter

Directions

1. Get a mixing bowl: Stir in the water with yeast and let them sit for 8 to 10 min until the yeast dissolves.
2. Add the sugar with flour, milk, salt and egg to the bowl and mix them well until your get a soft dough.
3. Transfer the dough to a floured surface. Knead it for 10 min. Transfer the dough to a greased bowl and cover it with a plastic wrap.
4. Place the aside and let it rise for about 60 min.
5. Once the time is up, place the dough on a floured surface and add to it the garlic. Knead it for few minutes.
6. Shape the dough into small golf size balls and place them on a lined up cookie sheet.
7. Place the dough sheet aside and let it rest for 32 min.
8. Before you do anything else, preheat the grill and grease it.
9. Place 1 dough ball on a slightly floured surface and flatten it until it becomes thin.
10. Place the dough circle over the greased grill and cook it for 2 to 4 min on each side.
11. Brush it completely with some melted butter then cook it for an extra 2 to 3 min on each side.
12. Repeat the process with the remaining dough.
13. Enjoy.

LENTIL
Feta Salad

🥣 Prep Time: 40 mins
🕒 Total Time: 1 hr 10 mins

Servings per Recipe: 4
Calories   378.1
Fat   30.2g
Cholesterol   40.1mg
Sodium   515.4mg
Carbohydrates   17.0g
Protein   11.5g

Ingredients

1 C. lentils
4 C. water
3/4 C. red pepper, chopped
1/3 C. red onion, chopped
2 tbsp of mint, chopped
6 tbsp olive oil
6 tbsp lemon juice

2 cloves garlic, minced
6 oz. feta cheese, crumbled

Directions

1. Place a large saucepan over medium heat. Stir in it the water with lentils and cook them until they start boiling.
2. Lower the heat and let them cook for an extra 35 min.
3. Once the time is up, pour the lentils in a fine mesh strainer and drain it completely.
4. Get a large mixing bowl: Place in it the lentils with onion, mint and pepper. Toss them to coat.
5. Place the salad in the fridge for 35 min.
6. Once the time is up, add to it the oil with lemon juice, deta and garlic. Mix them well then serve your salad right away.
7. Enjoy.

Chickpea Falafels

Prep Time: 15 mins
Total Time: 50 mins

Servings per Recipe: 1
Calories	37.9
Fat	0.8g
Cholesterol	9.3mg
Sodium	166.4mg
Carbohydrates	6.2g
Protein	1.6g

Ingredients

- 10.5 oz. chickpeas
- 4 tbsp bulgur
- 3 garlic cloves
- 3 tbsp plain flour
- 1 egg
- 1 tsp salt
- 1 tsp pepper
- 3 tsp ground coriander
- 1 tsp cumin
- 1/4 tsp ground red chili pepper
- 1 tbsp tahini

Directions

1. Get a large bowl of water. Place in it the chickpeas and let them sit for at least 12 h
2. Get a mixing bowl: Stir in it the bulghur with water and put on a lid to cover it. Let it sit for 1 h.
3. Place a large saucepan of water over medium heat. Cook in it the chickpeas for 22 min.
4. Get a blender: Place in the chickpeas after draining them. Blend them smooth.
5. Get a mixing bowl: Combine in it the chickpeas paste with burghul, garlic and salt. Mix them well.
6. Shape the mixture into medium size patties
7. Place a large pan over medium heat. Heat in it a splash of oil.
8. Add to it the falafels and cook them for 2 to 3 min on each side until they become golden brown.
9. Serve your falafels with some plain yogurt.
10. Enjoy.

HOMEMADE
Lebanese Pita Bread

Prep Time: 5 mins
Total Time: 46 mins

Servings per Recipe: 12
Calories   181.8
Fat   4.7g
Cholesterol   0.0mg
Sodium   292.5mg
Carbohydrates   30.0g
Protein   4.2g

Ingredients

1 (1/4 oz.) package active dry yeast
3 3/4 C. flour
1/4 C. shortening, softened
1 1/2 tsp salt
1 1/4 C. water

Directions

1. Before you do anything, preheat the oven to 350 F. Line up a baking sheet.
2. Get a mixing bowl: Stir in it the yeast with water and let them sit for 8 min.
3. Add to them 2 C. flour, shortening and salt. Mix them well using a hand mixer for 4 min.
4. Transfer the mixture to a working surface and add to it the remaining four while kneading it until it become soft.
5. Wrap the dough in a plastic wrap or damp towel. Place it aside and let it sit for 16 min
6. Once the time is up, divide the dough into 6 balls. Place them on a lined up cookie sheet and cover them with a damp cloth.
7. Let the dough balls rest for an extra 11 min.
8. Place 1 dough ball on a floured surface and flatten it into a 6 inches circle.
9. Place it in the lined up baking sheet and cook it in the oven for 3 to 4 min.
10. Flip the bread loaf and bake it for 2 to 2 min on the other side.
11. Place the bread loaf on a kitchen towel and cover it with another. Repeat the process with the remaining dough balls.
12. Serve your pita bread with some hummus or whatever you desire.
13. Enjoy.

Spicy Bread

Prep Time: 1 hr
Total Time: 1 hr 10 mins

Servings per Recipe: 1	
Calories	399.2
Fat	17.2g
Cholesterol	31.0mg
Sodium	790.4mg
Carbohydrates	52.5g
Protein	8.0g

Ingredients

- 2 tsp active dry yeast
- 1 egg, beaten
- 8 oz. tepid water
- 7 tbsp olive oil
- 2 tbsp sugar
- 2 tsp salt
- 3 C. unbleached white flour
- 2 - 3 tbsp za'atar spice mix

Directions

1. Get a mixing bowl: Stir in it the yeast with 3 tbsp of water.
2. Mix in it the egg with 4 tbsp of olive oil and sugar.
3. Get another mixing bowl: Stir in it the flour with salt. Add to them the water yeast mix and remaining water then combine them until you get a smooth dough.
4. Transfer the dough to a floured surface and knead it until it becomes soft.
5. Place the dough in a greased bowl and cover it with a plastic wrap. Let it rest for 46 min.
6. Before you do anything else, preheat the oven to 450 F.
7. Divide the dough into two pieces and shape each one of them into a ball. Place them on a lined up baking sheet.
8. Cover the dough balls with a kitchen towel then let them rest for 16 min.
9. Get a small mixing bowl: Mix it the za'atar with 3 tbsp of olive oil. Coat the bread balls with it.
10. Place the bread pan in the oven and cook them for 11 min until they become golden brown.
11. Allow the bread loaves to cool down completely then serve them and enjoy.
12. Enjoy.

CRISPY
Sumac Eggs

🥣 Prep Time: 5 mins
🕐 Total Time: 15 mins

Servings per Recipe: 3
Calories   262.3
Fat   23.0g
Cholesterol   372.0mg
Sodium   142.2mg
Carbohydrates   0.7g
Protein   12.5g

Ingredients

3 tbsp olive oil
6 eggs
1/2-1 tbsp sumac

salt & pepper

Directions

1. Place a large pan over medium heat. Heat in it the oil.
2. Place in it the eggs then sprinkle over them the sumac with a pinch of salt and pepper.
3. Fry the eggs until they are done then serve them warm.
4. Enjoy.

Mediterranean Spicy Shawarma

Prep Time: 10 mins
Total Time: 40 mins

Servings per Recipe: 4
Calories   714.2
Fat   39.5g
Cholesterol   92.8mg
Sodium   465.0mg
Carbohydrates   51.2g
Protein   40.7g

Ingredients

- 1 tbsp ground coriander
- 1 tbsp ground cumin
- 1 tbsp ground cardamom
- 1 tbsp chili powder
- 1 tsp smoked paprika
- 1 tbsp grill seasoning
- 1 lemon, juice of, divided
- 2 large garlic cloves, grated
- 5 tbsp extra-virgin olive oil, divided
- 4 chicken breasts, boneless, skinless
- 1 large onion, sliced
- 1 red bell pepper, sliced
- 1 yellow bell pepper, sliced
- 1/4 C. tahini
- 1 1/2 C. Greek yogurt
- 4 pita bread

Directions

1. Preheat the grill and grease it.
2. Get a small mixing bowl: Mix in it the coriander, cumin, cardamom, chili powder, paprika and grill seasoning.
3. Add the juice half a lemon, 3 tbsp of olive oil and garlic. Mix them well until they become like a paste.
4. Coat the chicken with the spice mixture then grill them for 7 to 8 min on each side.
5. Remove the chicken pieces from the grill and let them sit for 2 min.
6. Place a large pan over medium heat. Heat in it 2 tbsp of olive oil. Cook in it the peppers with onion, a pinch of salt and pepper for 6 min.
7. Get a mixing bowl: Mix in the rest of the lemon juice, tahini, yogurt, a drizzle of olive oil and a pinch of salt to make the white sauce.
8. Heat the pita bread on the grill. Lay in them the chicken pieces followed by the onion and pepper mixture.
9. Drizzle the yogurt sauce on top then serve them.
10. Enjoy.

SPICY CHICKEN and Nutty Rice Skillet

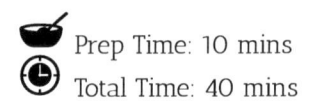

Prep Time: 10 mins
Total Time: 40 mins

Servings per Recipe: 4
Calories   645.9
Fat   27.5g
Cholesterol   108.2mg
Sodium   552.3mg
Carbohydrates   63.7g
Protein   33.8g

Ingredients

- 3 tbsp olive oil
- 4 boneless skinless chicken thighs
- 2 diced onions
- 10.5 oz. ground beef
- 1 tbsp minced garlic
- 2 tsp ground cinnamon
- 1 tsp ground allspice
- 1/4 tsp ground cayenne pepper
- 3/4 tsp salt
- 1 1/2 C. long grain rice
- 3 C. hot stock
- 2 tbsp pine nuts
- 2 tbsp minced parsley

Directions

1. Place a large skillet over medium heat. Heat in it the olive oil. Add the chicken thighs and cook it for 4 to 6 min on each side.
2. Drain them and place them aside. Cook the beef with onion in the same skillet for 7 min.
3. Stir in the garlic and cook them for an extra minute.
4. Mix in the cinnamon, allspice, cayenne pepper and salt. Cook them for 3 min.
5. Add the rice and mix them well. Place the chicken thighs on top followed by the pine nuts
6. Drizzle the stock all over them then put on the lid and let them cook for 35 min.
7. Once the time is up, serve your chicken and rice skillet warm.
8. Enjoy.

Spicy Beef and Spinach Rice Stew

Prep Time: 15 mins
Total Time: 1 hr

Servings per Recipe: 8
Calories   162.2
Fat   9.1g
Cholesterol   38.5mg
Sodium   119.0mg
Carbohydrates   6.6g
Protein   14.7g

Ingredients

olive oil
1 medium onion, diced
1 lb. ground beef
1 1/2 tsp allspice
1/2 tsp ground cinnamon
salt
30 oz. of frozen chopped spinach
water
3 garlic cloves, minced
1 bunch cilantro, chopped
lemon juice
rice, cooked

Directions

1. Place a large pot over medium heat and heat in it the oil.
2. Cook in it the onion for 3 min. Mix in the beef and cook them for 5 min.
3. Stir in the allspice with cinnamon and a pinch of salt. Mix them well.
4. Mix in the spinach and cook them for 3 min. Stir in the water and put on the lid.
5. Bring them to a rolling boil for 35 min over low medium heat.
6. Place a large skillet over medium heat. Heat in it the olive oil. Add the garlic with cilantro and cook them for 2 min.
7. Stir them into the beef pot. Put on the lid and cook them for 16 min.
8. Serve your spinach and beef stew warm with some rice.
9. Enjoy.

BROKEN HEARTS
Salad

Prep Time: 10 mins
Total Time: 10 mins

Servings per Recipe: 6
Calories   20.2
Fat   0.3g
Cholesterol   0.0mg
Sodium   9.6mg
Carbohydrates   4.0g
Protein   1.4g

Ingredients

1 head romaine lettuce
3 - 4 scallions, chopped
2 - 3 tbsp chopped dill

olive oil
vinegar
salt

Directions

1. Finely chop the lettuce leaves.
2. Toss them in a large mixing bowl with dill, scallions, a drizzle of olive oil, vinegar and a pinch of salt.
3. Serve your salad right away.
4. Enjoy.

Red Bean Salad

Prep Time: 2 hrs
Total Time: 2 hrs 5 mins

Servings per Recipe:	4
Calories	107.7
Fat	7.0g
Cholesterol	0.0mg
Sodium	154.5mg
Carbohydrates	10.9g
Protein	2.4g

Ingredients

- 1 lb. green beans, washed and ends trimmed
- 1/2 C. chopped red onion
- 2 tbsp chopped parsley
- 2 garlic cloves, minced
- 2 tbsp lemon juice
- 2 tbsp olive oil
- 1/4 tsp pepper
- 1/4 tsp salt

Directions

1. Place the green beans in a steamer and cook them for 6 min.
2. Get a large mixing bowl: Toss in it the beans with the remaining ingredients.
3. Place the salad in the fridge and let it sit for at least 120 min then serve it.
4. Enjoy.

NAVY
Beans Soup

🍲 Prep Time: 5 mins
🕐 Total Time: 50 mins

Servings per Recipe: 7
Calories   391.6
Fat   31.4g
Cholesterol   0.0mg
Sodium   369.9mg
Carbohydrates   23.2g
Protein   6.3

Ingredients

1 lb. navy beans
3 carrots, peeled and sliced
1 onion, peeled and chopped
3 stalks celery, chopped
1 C. tomato sauce

1 C. olive oil
salt
pepper

Directions

1. Get a mixing bowl: Place in it the beans and cover them with water. Let it sit for 8 h.
2. Drain it the beans and place it in a large pot. Cover it with cool down and bring it to a boil.
3. Stir into it the remaining ingredients. Put on the lid and let them cook for 60 min over low heat.
4. Serve your beans soup warm.
5. Enjoy.

Lebanese Meatloaf Rolls

🥣 Prep Time: 30 mins
🕒 Total Time: 3 hrs 30 mins

Servings per Recipe: 1
Calories   1983.8
Fat   79.8g
Cholesterol   477.1mg
Sodium   1464.7mg
Carbohydrates   159.6g
Protein   151.0g

Ingredients

FOR MEATLOAF
3 lbs. lean hamburger
3/4 C. breadcrumbs
2 tsp pepper
1 - 2 tsp red cayenne pepper
1 1/2 tsp oregano
3 tsp paprika
2 tsp onion powder
1 tsp garlic powder
1/2 tsp salt

FOR SAUCE
2/3 C. canned milk
2/3 C. sugar
2 tbsp white vinegar
1/2 tsp garlic powder

FOR SANDWICH
pita bread
chopped onion
sliced tomatoes

Directions

1. Before you do anything, preheat the oven to 300 F.
2. To make the meatloaf: Get a large mixing bowl: Mix in it all the meatloaf ingredients with your hands for 18 min. Divide the mix into the 2 portions and shape them into loaves.
3. Place the meatloaves in a roasting pan. Cook them in the oven for 2 h 20 min.
4. Once the time is up, allow the meatloaves to cool down completely. Cut the meatloaves into thin slices then place them aside.
5. To make the sauce:
6. Place a heavy saucepan over medium heat. Combine in it the milk, sugar and garlic powder Cook them while stirring all the time until the sugar melts. Pour in the vinegar and keep mixing them until for 2 to 3 min.
7. Place the sauce aside to cool down for 60 min.
8. Place a large pan over medium heat. Heat in it some of meatloaves slices.
9. Spread some of the sauce it in the bread rolls; top it with the meatloaf slices followed by the onion and tomato. Serve your sandwiches and enjoy. Enjoy.

LEMON
Lentils Soup

Prep Time: 15 mins
Total Time: 45 mins

Servings per Recipe: 8
Calories   152.6
Fat   7.0g
Cholesterol   0.0mg
Sodium   81.2mg
Carbohydrates   16.4g
Protein   6.4g

Ingredients

1 C. large green lentils
1 bunch Swiss chard, chopped
7 C. water
10 garlic cloves, peeled and crushed
1/4 tsp salt

2 lemons, juice
1/4 C. extra virgin olive oil

Directions

1. Place a large saucepan over water over high heat. Stir into it the lentils and cook them until they start boiling.
2. Lower the heat and put on the lid. Cook them for 40 min. Add to it the chard and cook them for 8 min.
3. Get a mortar and pestle: Place in it the garlic with a pinch of salt. Crush them until they become like a paste.
4. Add to it the olive oil with lemon juice and mix them well.
5. Stir the mixture into the soup with a pinch of salt and pepper. Cook the soup for an extra 6 min then serve it hot.
6. Enjoy.

Nutty Lebanese Kebaa

Prep Time: 30 mins
Total Time: 1 hr

Servings per Recipe: 8
Calories   378.4
Fat   30.1g
Cholesterol   73.7mg
Sodium   374.8mg
Carbohydrates   11.1g
Protein   16.5g

Ingredients

- 1 C. Bulgar wheat
- 1 1/2 lbs. lean ground lamb
- 1/2 C. pine nuts
- 4 medium onions, minced
- 3 tbsp butter
- 1 tsp pepper
- 1 tsp salt
- 1/8 tsp allspice
- 1/8 tsp clove

Directions

1. Get a mixing bowl: Place in it the bulgar wheat and cover it with water. Let it sit for 60 min then drain it.
2. Before you do anything, preheat the oven to 400 F. Grease a casserole dish.
3. Place a large pan over medium heat. Cook in it the onions with pine nuts for 3 min.
4. Get a large mixing bowl: Mix in it the meat, wheat, and spices. Mix them well.
5. Split the mixture into 1 portion. Spread one portion in the bottom of the greased casserole dish.
6. Spread over it the onion mixture followed by the remaining meat mixture.
7. Dip a knife in some water then cut the kebba casserole into squares or diamond shapes.
8. Place the kebaa casserole in the oven and bake it for 28 min. Serve it warm with some sour cream.
9. Enjoy.

HOMEMADE
Oregano Pizza

🥣 Prep Time: 5 mins
🕐 Total Time: 20 mins

Servings per Recipe: 1
Calories   595.0
Fat   39.2g
Cholesterol   98.7mg
Sodium   2506.5mg
Carbohydrates   33.2g
Protein   34.0g

Ingredients

3.5oz. Lebanese bread
4.5 oz. tomato paste
4.5 oz. mozzarella cheese, grated
3.5oz. Kalamata olives
1/4 tsp dried oregano

1/4 tsp dried basil
1/4 tsp ground black pepper

Directions

1. Before you do anything, preheat the oven to 425 F. Grease a baking pan.
2. Place the Lebanese bread on the baking pan. Lay over it the tomato paste followed by mozzarella, and olives.
3. Sprinkle the dry oregano, basil, and a pinch of black pepper on top.
4. Place the pizza in the oven and bake cook it for 12 to 16 min. Serve it warm.
5. Enjoy.

Summer Hearts Soup

Prep Time: 15 mins
Total Time: 35 mins

Servings per Recipe: 8
Calories 191.4
Fat 4.2g
Cholesterol 0.0mg
Sodium 884.8mg
Carbohydrates 37.1g
Protein 8.2g

Ingredients

1 large Spanish onion, chopped
2 tbsp olive oil
2 1/2 C. chopped carrots
1/4 tsp ground red pepper
1 tsp ground coriander
2 - 4 garlic cloves, minced
1 1/2 C. chopped potatoes
1 tsp salt

4 - 5 C. vegetable stock
2 large tomatoes, chopped
10 artichoke hearts, chopped
3/4 C. canned chickpeas
1/4 C. chopped parsley
2 lemons, wedges

Directions

1. Get a large jug: Mix in it the vegetable stock, the chick pea liquid and the artichoke heart brine to make the stock.
2. Place a large pot over medium heat. Heat in it the oil. Add the onion and cook it for 6 min.
3. Add to it the carrots. Put on the lid and cook them for 4 min.
4. Stir in the ground red pepper, coriander, and garlic. Put on the lid and cook them for 4 min.
5. Stir in the potato with 2 C. of the stock and a pinch of salt. Put on the lid and cook them until they start boiling.
6. Lower the heat and let the soup cook for 20 min. Add the tomatoes, artichoke hearts, and the chick peas.
7. Put on the lid and cook them for 5 min. Stir in 3 C. of stock then let the soup cook for an extra 6 min.
8. Adjust the seasoning of the soup then serve it warm.
9. Enjoy.

GOLDEN Roasted Chicken

Prep Time: 1 hr 10 mins
Total Time: 2 hrs 25 mins

Servings per Recipe: 6
Calories   1469.3
Fat   109.1g
Cholesterol   454.0mg
Sodium   424.5mg
Carbohydrates   2.7g
Protein   112.8g

Ingredients

2 (4 lb.) broiler-fryer chickens, in pieces
1/2-3/4 C. olive oil
2/3 C. lemon juice
2 tbsp thyme
1 tsp garlic powder

Directions

1. Get a mixing bowl: Mix it the olive oil with lemon juice, thyme and garlic powder to make the marinade.
2. Add to it the chicken pieces and toss them to coat. Place the marinated chicken pieces in the fridge and let them sit for 60 min.
3. Before you do anything, preheat the oven to 350 F.
4. Drain the chicken pieces and place them in a roasting pan. Cook them in the oven for 65 min.
5. Enjoy.

Sumac Spring Salad

Prep Time:	15 mins
Total Time:	15 mins

Servings per Recipe: 4
Calories 113.6
Fat 7.3g
Cholesterol 0.0mg
Sodium 25.7mg
Carbohydrates 11.5g
Protein 2.5g

Ingredients

1 carrot, chopped
1/2 cos lettuce, chopped
1 cucumber, chopped
2 tomatoes, chopped
5 radishes, chopped
1 tbsp spring onions, chopped
1 red capsicums, chopped
1 garlic clove, chopped
1 tbsp flat leaf parsley, chopped
2 tsp ground sumac
1 large flat bread, toasted and broken into pieces
2 - 3 tbsp olive oil
salt

Directions

1. Get a small mixing bowl: Whisk in it the garlic, parsley, sumac, bread, olive oil and salt.
2. Get a large mixing bowl: Combine in it the remaining ingredients. Add the oil dressing and mix them well.
3. Serve your salad right away.
4. Enjoy.

CLASSIC
Minty Lebanese Tabbouli

Prep Time: 1 hr
Total Time: 1 hr

Servings per Recipe: 6
Calories   218.3
Fat   18.4g
Cholesterol   0.0mg
Sodium   14.4mg
Carbohydrates   13.6g
Protein   2.5g

Ingredients

1 C. medium Bulgar wheat
2 -3 bunches parsley, stemmed and chopped
1 -2 bunch mint leaves, chopped
4 -5 ripe firm tomatoes, seeded and chopped

3 -5 lemons, juice
1/2 C. extra virgin olive oil
salt & ground pepper

Directions

1. Get a mixing bowl: Toss in it all the ingredients. Place it in the fridge and let it sit for 60 min.
2. Serve your salad with some bread stick.
3. Enjoy.

Homemade Flat Lebanese Bread

🥣 Prep Time: 1 hr
🕒 Total Time: 1 hr 5 mins

Servings per Recipe: 1
Calories   375.9
Fat   4.3g
Cholesterol   0.0mg
Sodium   439.5mg
Carbohydrates   72.4g
Protein   10.0g

Ingredients

6 C. flour
1 package active dry yeast
2 C. warm water
1 1/2 tsp salt
1 tsp sugar
2 tbsp oil

Directions

1. Get a mixing bowl: Stir in it the 1/4 C. of warm water with yeast.
2. Stir in the rest of the water with salt and sugar until they dissolve.
3. Get a large mixing bowl: Mix in it 4 C. of flour with the yeast mixture until you get a thick batter.
4. Lay a plastic wrap over the bowl to cover it. let it rest until it becomes frothy.
5. Once the time is up, add the remaining flour with oil then mix them well for 9 min until your get a smooth dough.
6. Transfer the dough to a floured surface and knead it for 11 min.
7. Place the dough ball in a greased bowl and coat it with some oil. Lay over it a plastic wrap to cover it.
8. Let the dough rest for 1 h 15 min.
9. Before you do anything, preheat the oven to 500 F.
10. Place the dough on a floured surface. knead it for 2 min then shape it into 8 balls.
11. Flatten each dough ball on a floured surface until it becomes 10 inches round.
12. Place them on a piece of cloth and cover them with another. Let them rest for 25 min.
13. Place the dough circles in greased baking sheets. Cook them in the oven for 4 to 6 min or until they are done.
14. Allow the flat bread to cool down completely then serve them.
15. Enjoy.

ROSY
Almonds Pudding

🥣 Prep Time: 10 mins]
🕐 Total Time: 25 mins

Servings per Recipe: 6
Calories 202.7
Fat 10.4g
Cholesterol 17.0mg
Sodium 85.8mg
Carbohydrates 21.8g
Protein 6.9g

Ingredients

1/4 C. rice flour
3 C. milk
1 pinch salt
1/4 C. sugar
3/4 C. ground almonds

1 tbsp rose water
pistachios

Directions

1. Get a blender: Combine in it 1/4 C. of milk with the ground rice. Blend them smooth.
2. Place a heavy saucepan over medium heat. Heat in it the remaining milk until it starts boiling.
3. Add to it the rice mix with sugar and a pinch of salt. Cook it until it starts boiling while stirring it all the time.
4. Let the rice pudding cook for 5 to 6 min until it becomes creamy.
5. Lower the heat then fold the almonds with rosewater into the pudding.
6. Allow it to cool down for a while then serve it with your favorite toppings.
7. Enjoy.

Nutty Short Cookies

Prep Time: 30 mins
Total Time: 40 mins

Servings per Recipe: 50
Calories	67.5
Fat	4.5g
Cholesterol	10.7mg
Sodium	12.8mg
Carbohydrates	6.3g
Protein	0.6g

Ingredients

- 2 C. flour
- 2 tsp ground cardamom
- 1 C. pure ghee
- 1 C. icing sugar
- 50 blanched almond halves
- 1/2 tsp baking soda

Directions

1. Before you do anything, preheat the oven to 350 F. Grease a baking pan.
2. Place a heavy saucepan over medium heat. Stir in it the sugar with ghee until they melt.
3. Turn off the heat. Mix in the cardamom followed by the flour and baking soda gradually until you get a smooth dough.
4. Place 1 tsp of dough in your hands and roll it into a ball. Press it slightly with the palm of your hands to flatten it.
5. Place it on a lined up baking sheet. Repeat the process with the remaining dough.
6. Place an almond in the middle of each cookie. Bake the cookies for 11 min. Allow them to cool down completely then serve them.
7. Enjoy.

GOLDEN RICE and Raisins Pudding

Prep Time: 5 mins
Total Time: 30 mins

Servings per Recipe: 4
Calories   431.3
Fat   7.4g
Cholesterol   0.0mg
Sodium   156.5mg
Carbohydrates 83.2g
Protein   7.0g

Ingredients

2 C. long grain white rice
4 C. water
1/4 C. golden raisin
1/4-1/2 tsp salt
1 1/2 tbsp cinnamon
1/8 C. olive oil
1/2 tsp saffron
plain yogurt

Directions

1. Stir 2 C. of rice with 4 C. of water in a rice maker.
2. Stir into it the raisins, cinnamon, saffron, a drizzle of olive oil and a pinch of salt.
3. Follow the manufacturer's instructions to cook the rice.
4. Allow the rice pudding to cool down for a while then serve it with some yogurt.
5. Enjoy.

Shawarma Pie

Prep Time: 20 mins
Total Time: 1 hr

Servings per Recipe: 8
Calories   387.8
Fat   14.5g
Cholesterol   68.8mg
Sodium   601.3mg
Carbohydrates   42.4g
Protein   24.7g

Ingredients

- 2 lbs. sweet potatoes, peeled and quartered
- 1 lb. ground turkey
- 1 large onion, diced
- 1/2 tsp ground cinnamon
- 1/2 tsp salt
- 1/2 tsp pepper
- 1/4 tsp ground cloves
- 1/4 tsp ground nutmeg
- 1/4 tsp ground cardamom
- 1/4 tsp ground ginger
- 1 C. beef broth
- 2 tsp Worcestershire sauce
- 32 oz. frozen mixed vegetables
- 2 C. sharp cheddar cheese, shredded

Directions

1. Bring a large salted pot of water to a boil. Cook in it the potatoes for 20 to 25 min until they become soft.
2. Drain the potatoes then mash them with butter and a splash of milk.
3. Place a large pan over medium heat. Cook in it the beef for 8 min.
4. Stir into it the onion, seasonings, beef broth and Worcestershire sauce. Cook them for 12 min over low heat.
5. Turn off the heat and to it the frozen veggies. Pour the mixture into a greased baking dish.
6. Sprinkle the cheese over it then top it with the mashed potato. Place the pan in the oven and cook it for 52 min.
7. Serve your shawarma pie warm.
8. Enjoy.

CRISPY Zucchini Salad

Prep Time: 15 mins
Total Time: 4 hrs 15 mins

Servings per Recipe: 6
Calories 107.8
Fat 9.2g
Cholesterol 0.0mg
Sodium 13.0mg
Carbohydrates 5.6g
Protein 1.7g

Ingredients

4 tbsp olive oil
1 small head of garlic, peeled and sliced
1 1/2 lbs. zucchini, sliced
4 tbsp vinegar
salt and pepper

2 tbsp green onions, chopped
1/8 tsp cayenne
2 tbsp cilantro, chopped

Directions

1. Place a large pan over medium heat. Heat in it the oil.
2. Add the garlic and cook it for 30 sec. Drain it and place it aside.
3. Add the zucchini slices to the pan and cook them for 1 to 2 min on each side until they become golden brown.
4. Get a mixing bowl: Whisk in it the vinegar with green onion, cayenne pepper, cilantro, cooked garlic, a pinch of salt and pepper.
5. Lay the fried zucchini slices on a serving plate. Drizzle over it the parsley mixture.
6. Place the salad in the fridge and let it sit for at least 3 h then serve it.
7. Enjoy.

Hummus Boats

Prep Time: 5 mins
Total Time: 20 mins

Servings per Recipe: 6
Calories   68.2
Fat   3.0g
Cholesterol   0.0mg
Sodium   171.3mg
Carbohydrates   4.6g
Protein   6.0g

Ingredients

6 egg whites, hard boiled peeled and cut lengthwise
3/4 C. hummus
parsley
paprika
slivered almonds

Directions

1. Place the egg yolks in a mixing bowl and use them for another recipe.
2. Place the hummus in a piping bag. Fill with it the egg whites.
3. Place them on a serving plate. Garnish your hummus boats with some parsley, paprika, or almonds.
4. Enjoy.

BEEF LOAF
with Yogurt

🥣 Prep Time: 30 mins
🕐 Total Time: 55 mins

Servings per Recipe: 4
Calories   263.6
Fat   6.0g
Cholesterol   71.4mg
Sodium   712.1mg
Carbohydrates   21.5g
Protein   30.2g

Ingredients

1 C. Bulgar wheat, rinsed
2 C. coarsely chopped onions
1 lb. extra lean ground beef
1/2 tsp pepper
1/2 tsp ground cumin
1/2 tsp ground cinnamon

1 tsp salt
1/3 C. chopped parsley
black peppercorns
1 C. plain nonfat yogurt

Directions

1. Before you do anything, preheat the oven to 425 F. Grease a baking dish.
2. Get a blender: Combine in it the onion with beef, 1/2 C. water, pepper, cumin, cinnamon, and 1 tsp salt. Mix them well.
3. Mix in the bulgur and 1/4 C. parsley. Pour the mixture into the greased pan. Spread it in an even layer.
4. Wet a knife with some water. Slice the meatloaf into diamonds shape. Press each peppercorn into each diamond.
5. Place the pan in the oven and cook them for 26 min.
6. Garnish the meatloaf diamonds with some parsley then serve it with some yogurt.
7. Enjoy.

Sumac Bread

🥣 Prep Time: 55 mins
🕐 Total Time: 1 hr 20 mins

Servings per Recipe: 4
Calories   502.6
Fat   34.6g
Cholesterol   622.9mg
Sodium   42.0g
Carbohydrates   5.9g
Protein   4.0g

Ingredients

FOR THE DOUGH
1/2 tsp active dry yeast
1/2 C. warm water, divided
1 3/4 C. all-purpose flour
1 tsp salt
2 tbsp vegetable oil
FOR THE TOPPING

2 tbsp powdered thyme
1 tbsp sumac
3/4 tsp sesame seeds
1 dash salt
1/2 C. extra virgin olive oil
1 small onion, chopped

Directions

1. To make the dough:
2. Stir the yeast with 1/4 C. of warm water and let them sit for 8 min.
3. Get a large mixing bowl: Mix in it the flour with oil and a pinch of salt. Mix them well.
4. Add the yeast mixture and mix them well. Add 1/4 C. of warm water and mix them until you get a smooth dough.
5. Shape the dough into a ball and place it in a greased bowl. Cover it with a plastic wrap and let it sit for 60 min.
6. To make the topping:
7. Get a mixing bowl: Combine in it all the topping ingredients.
8. Shape the dough into 4 balls. Dredge a ball of dough in some flour then flatten into a 1/8 inch thick circle.
9. Place a large pan over medium heat. Brush the dough with the topping mixture.
10. Place it in the pan and let it cook for 4 to 6 min until the edges becomes golden brown.
11. Repeat the process with the remaining dough and topping.
12. Allow the bread loaves to cool down completely. Serve it with your favorite dip.
13. Enjoy.

SUMMER
Lentils Pilaf

Prep Time: 35 mins
Total Time: 50 mins

Servings per Recipe: 6
Calories 232.6
Fat 3.1g
Cholesterol 0.0mg
Sodium 532.3mg
Carbohydrates 40.9g
Protein 12.3g

Ingredients

4 C. fat-free chicken broth
1 C. medium grain bulgur
1 C. brown lentils, rinsed and picked over
1 medium onion, coarse chopped
1 bay leaf
1/2 tsp salt
1/2 tsp allspice
1/2 tsp black pepper
1 tbsp lemon juice

1 tbsp olive oil
1 small zucchini
1 small yellow squash
1 garlic clove, minced
1 tsp lemon zest, grated
1 1/2 tbsp parsley, chopped
1 tbsp cilantro, chopped
lemon wedge

Directions

1. Place a pot over medium heat. Stir in it the broth, lentils, onion bay leaf, salt allspice and pepper.
2. Cook them until they start boiling. Lower the heat and put on the lid. Cook them for 11 min.
3. Once the time is up, stir in the bulgur and let it cook for an extra 26 min.
4. Turn off the heat and add the lemon juice.
5. Place a large pan over medium heat. Heat in it the oil. Cook in it the zucchini and squash for 3 min.
6. Stir in the garlic with lemon zest. Cook them for 2 min. Fold the parsley with cilantro, a pinch of salt and pepper into the mix.
7. Add the zucchini mix into the lentils pot. Fluff it with a fork then serve your pilaf warm.
8. Enjoy.

Creamy Steak Baguettes

> Prep Time: 5 hrs
> Total Time: 5 hrs 5 mins

Servings per Recipe: 4
Calories   1005.8
Fat   23.5g
Cholesterol   53.5mg
Sodium   1557.7mg
Carbohydrates   156.2g
Protein   43.1g

Ingredients

1/2 lb. sliced New York strip steaks
1 baguette
4 tomatoes
1 (6 oz.) packages garlic and herb goat cheese
1/2 C. regular mayonnaise

MARINADE
cumin
extra virgin olive oil
garlic salt
paprika

Directions

1. To make the dough:
2. Stir the yeast with 1/4 C. of warm water and let them sit for 8 min.
3. Get a large mixing bowl: Mix in it the flour with oil and a pinch of salt. Mix them well.
4. Add the yeast mixture and mix them well. Add 1/4 C. of warm water and mix them until you get a smooth dough.
5. Shape the dough into a ball and place it in a greased bowl. Cover it with a plastic wrap and let it sit for 60 min.
6. To make the topping:
7. Get a mixing bowl: Combine in it all the topping ingredients.
8. Shape the dough into 4 balls. Dredge a ball of dough in some flour then flatten into a 1/8 inch thick circle.
9. Place a large pan over medium heat. Brush the dough with the topping mixture.
10. Place it in the pan and let it cook for 4 to 6 min until the edges becomes golden brown.
11. Repeat the process with the remaining dough and topping.
12. Allow the bread loaves to cool down completely. Serve it with your favorite dip.
13. Enjoy.

MIDNIGHT
Lemon Salad

Prep Time: 15 mins
Total Time: 15 mins

Servings per Recipe: 4
Calories 52.2
Fat 1.5g
Cholesterol 0.0mg
Sodium 14.3mg
Carbohydrates 8.8g
Protein 2.4g

Ingredients

1 (5 oz.) boxes baby arugula, rinsed
2 sweet white onions, sliced
1 C. chopped mushroom
1 tomatoes, diced
1 tsp extra virgin olive oil

1/2 lemon, juiced
2 tsp sumac
sea salt

Directions

1. Lay the aurgual oon a serving plate. Top it with the onions, mushrooms and tomato.
2. Get a small mixing bowl: Mix in it the olive oil, lemon juice, sumac, a pinch of salt and pepper.
3. Drizzle the vinaigrette over the salad. Serve it right away.
4. Enjoy.

Roasted Lemon Potato Casserole

Prep Time: 10 mins
Total Time: 50 mins

Servings per Recipe: 4
Calories	363.9
Fat	20.5g
Cholesterol	0.0mg
Sodium	15.8mg
Carbohydrates	43.5g
Protein	5.1g

Ingredients

- 1 lb. new potato, rinsed and diced
- 3 tbsp olive oil
- 2 garlic cloves, in their skins, crushed
- 1/2 lemon, juice
- 2 tbsp cilantro, chopped
- salt and pepper

Directions

1. Before you do anything, preheat the oven to 425 F.
2. Grease a casserole dish. Stir in the potato with olive oil, garlic, salt and pepper.
3. Place the casserole in the oven and cook them for 36 to 42 min.
4. Once the time is up, add the lemon juice with cilantro to the potato.
5. Stir it then serve it warm or cold with some yogurt.
6. Enjoy.

VERMICELLI
Rice

Prep Time: 5 mins
Total Time: 21 mins

Servings per Recipe: 4
Calories   209.6
Fat   4.5g
Cholesterol   11.4mg
Sodium   33.9mg
Carbohydrates   37.8g
Protein   3.2g

Ingredients

1 C. white rice
1/4 C. rice vermicelli
1 1/2 tbsp butter
water
sea salt

1/4-1/2 tsp cinnamo

Directions

1. Place a pot over medium heat. Heat in it the butter.
2. Cook in it the vermicelli and cook it for 2 to 3 min until it becomes golden brown.
3. Stir in the cinnamon with rice and 2 C. of water. Cook them until they start boiling.
4. Lower the heat and let the rice cook until it is done. Use a fork to fluff the vermicelli rice.
5. Serve it with some roasted chicken, tomato sauce or hummus.
6. Enjoy.

Crunchy Tomato and Cabbage Salad

Prep Time: 10 mins
Total Time: 20 mins

Servings per Recipe: 4
Calories	76.3
Fat	3.6g
Cholesterol	0.0mg
Sodium	318.6mg
Carbohydrates	10.5g
Protein	2.3g

Ingredients

- 1 lb. green cabbage, cored and sliced
- 2 tomatoes, chopped
- 1/3 C. parsley, chopped
- 1 tbsp lemon juice
- 1/3 C. scallion, diced
- 1 tsp garlic, minced
- 1/2 tsp salt
- 1/2 tsp ground pepper
- 1 tbsp olive oil

Directions

1. Get a large mixing bowl: Toss in it the cabbage with tomato, scallions and parsley.
2. Get a small mixing bowl: Mix in it the lemon juice, garlic, olive oil, and a pinch of salt.
3. Add the vinaigrette to the salad and stir it. Place it in the fridge for 11 min then serve it.
4. Enjoy.

BLUSHING
Tuna Salad

Prep Time: 10 mins
Total Time: 10 mins

Servings per Recipe: 4
Calories   433.7
Fat   35.6g
Cholesterol   24.8mg
Sodium   770.7mg
Carbohydrates   8.4g
Protein   23.0g

Ingredients

2 (160 g) cans tuna in olive oil
75 g chopped flat leaf parsley
1 1/2 tsp thyme
3 stalks green onions
2 - 3 ripe tomatoes, seeded and chopped
1/2 C. chopped olive
1 lemon
1/2 C. olive oil
1/2 tsp salt

Directions

1. Drain the tuna and flake it.
2. Get a large mixing bowl: Toss in it the tuna with salt, green or black olives, tomatoes, green onion, thyme, and parsley.
3. Get a small mixing bowl: Whisk in it the lemon juice with olive oil.
4. Add it to the salad and toss them to coat.
5. Place the salad in the fridge and let it sit for at least 60 min then serve it.
6. Enjoy.

Creamy Black Salad

🥣 Prep Time: 15 mins
🕐 Total Time: 55 mins

Servings per Recipe: 8
Calories	110.7
Fat	8.3g
Cholesterol	0.9mg
Sodium	138.2mg
Carbohydrates	9.4g
Protein	1.5g

Ingredients

- 2 large eggplants, peeled & cut into cubes
- 6 garlic cloves, peeled
- 1/4 C. vegetable oil
- 1/2 tsp kosher salt
- 2 - 3 tbsp mayonnaise

Directions

1. Before you do anything, preheat the oven to 425 F.
2. Stir in it thee garlic with eggplant disc, oil and a pinch of salt.
3. Place the pan in the oven and cook them for 22 min. Stir the eggplants dices then cook them for an extra 22 to 24 min.
4. Add the mayo to the baked eggplant and toss them to coat.
5. Allow the eggplant casserole to cool down completely then serve it.
6. Enjoy.

NUTTY Lamb Pierogis

Prep Time: 2 hr
Total Time: 2 hrs 20 mins

Servings per Recipe: 8
Calories 436.1
Fat 20.0g
Cholesterol 61.7mg
Sodium 343.7mg
Carbohydrates 46.8g
Protein 16.2g

Ingredients

JAMILAHS BASIC DOUGH
1 egg
1 (7 g) packets dry active yeast
1/4 C. war water
1 tsp sugar
3 1/2 C. all-purpose flour
1 tsp salt
1/4 C. extra virgin olive oil
2 tbsp extra virgin olive oil
1 1/4 C. warm milk
MEAT FILLING
1 tbsp olive oil
1 lb. coarsely ground lamb

1 medium onion, chopped
1/2 tsp ground cinnamon
1/2 tsp ground allspice
1/4 tsp black pepper
1/4 tsp white pepper
salt
1/4 C. pine nuts, sautéed in butter
1/2 C. chopped tomato
2 tbsp lemon juice
extra olive oil

Directions

1. To make the dough:
2. Get a large mixing bowl: Stir in it 1/4 C. of water with yeast. Let it sit for 8 to 9 min
3. Add to them the flour with salt, olive oil, egg, and warm milk. Mix them well until you get a soft dough.
4. Place the dough in a greased bowl and cover it with a wet kitchen towel. Let it rest for 120 min.
5. To make the Meat Filling:
6. Place a pan over medium heat. Heat in it the oil. Cook in it the lamb meat for 5 min.
7. Add the onion and cook them for an extra 6 min. Mix in the pine nuts with spices, a pinch of salt and pepper.
8. Cook them for 1 min while stirring them often. Stir in the tomato then put on the lid and

cook them for 14 to 16 min over low heat.
9. Turn off the heat and add the lemon juice. Place the filling aside to cool down.
10. Before you do anything, preheat the oven to 400 F.
11. Divide the dough into 8 balls. Flatten them on a floured surface into 4 inches circles.
12. Place 1/8 of the meat filling on one side of each dough circle. Pull the other side of the dough circle over the filling to cover it.
13. Press the edges with a fork to seal them. Place the lamb stuffed pierogis on a lined up baking sheet.
14. Place the pierogis pan in the oven and cook them for 19 to 21 min.
15. Serve your pierogis warm with your favorite dip.
16. Enjoy.

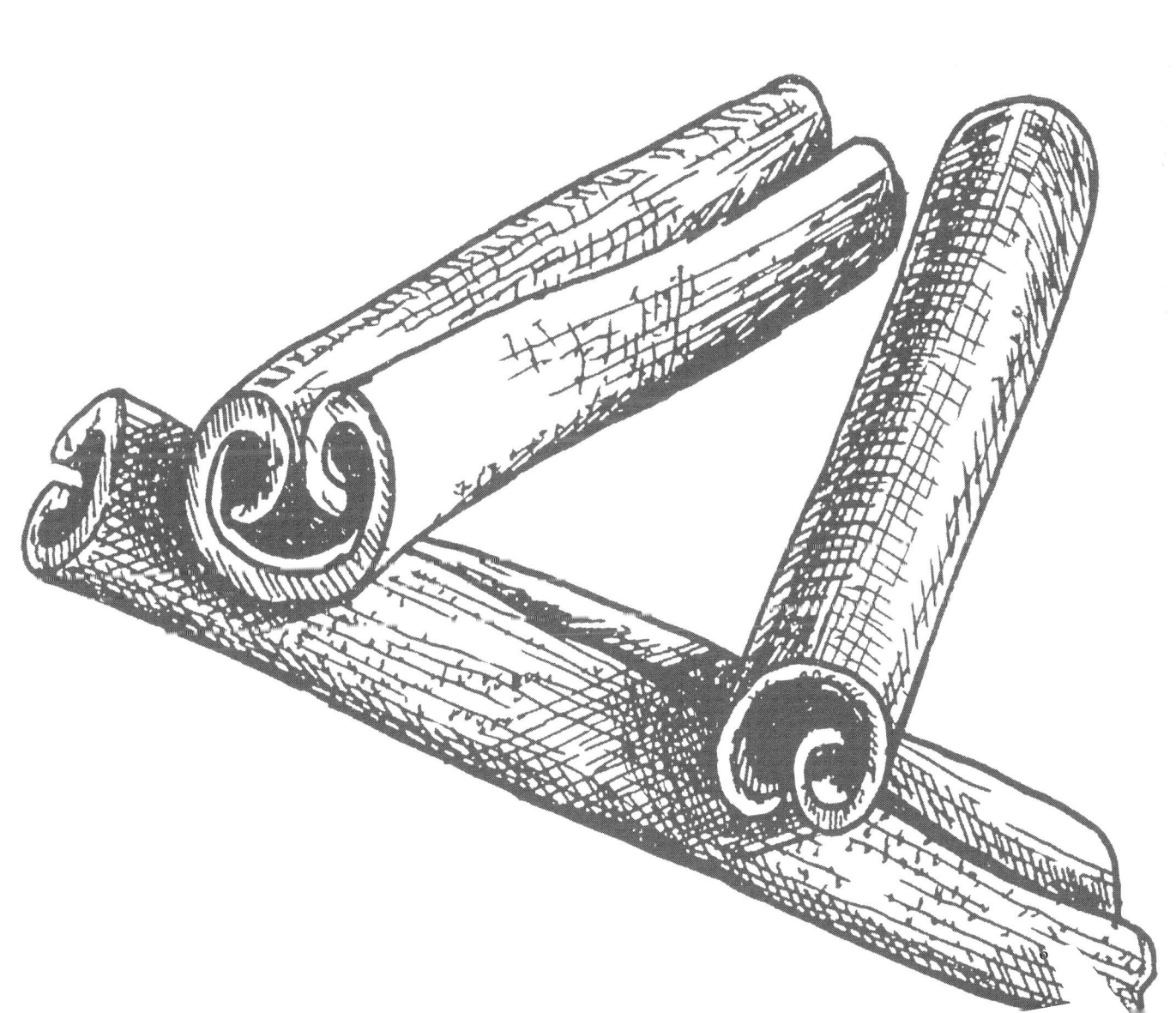

GOLDEN CAULIFLOWER
Bites with Tahini

🥣 Prep Time: 30 mins
⏱ Total Time: 1 hr 30 mins

Servings per Recipe: 4
Calories   214.9
Fat   14.8g
Cholesterol   0.0mg
Sodium   1813.3mg
Carbohydrates   17.1g
Protein   8.4g

Ingredients

FOR THE CAULIFLOWER
2 tsp salt
1 head cauliflower, cut into florets
canola oil
FOR THE TAHINI SAUCE
1 large garlic clove, crushed
1 tsp salt
1/2 C. tahini
1/3 C. lemon juice
1/4 C. water
1/4 C. chopped flat leaf parsley, use green leafy parts and tender stems

Directions

1. Place a pot over medium high heat. Het in it 8 C. of water with a pinch of salt.
2. Bring it to a rolling boil. Cook in it the cauliflower florets for 5 to 6 min.
3. Drain them and place them in fine mesh sieve to cool down completely.
4. Place a large skillet over medium heat. Heat in it 1 1/2 inch of oil.
5. Cook in it the cauliflower florets in batches until they become golden brown.
6. Drain them and place them on a lined up baking sheet.
7. Get a small mixing bowl: Mix in it all the tahini sauce ingredients.
8. Place the fried cauliflower florets on a serving plate. Drizzle over them the tahini sauce then serve them.
9. Enjoy.

Spicy Beef and Squash Skillet

🥣 Prep Time: 20 mins
🕐 Total Time: 1 hr 10 mins

Servings per Recipe: 2
Calories　　　　　753.7
Fat　　　　　　　51.0g
Cholesterol　　　　96.3mg
Sodium　　　　　147.5mg
Carbohydrates　　　47.9g
Protein　　　　　　32.2g

Ingredients

- 1 to 1 1/3 lb. butternut squash
- 2 tbsp olive oil
- sea salt
- fresh ground black pepper
- 1 medium onion, peeled and chopped
- 1/2 lb. ground beef
- 1 tsp cumin
- 1/2 tsp baharat
- 1 oz. pine nuts
- 1/4 C. water
- 1 oz. flat leaf parsley
- 6 oz. plain yogurt
- 1 plump garlic clove, chopped
- 1/2 tbsp lemon juice, freshly squeezed
- 1 tbsp extra virgin olive oil

Directions

1. Before you do anything, preheat the oven to 425 F. Grease a casserole dish. Slice the butternut squash in half and discard the seeds from it. Coat it with 1 tbsp of oil, a pinch of salt and pepper.
2. Place on a lined up baking sheet with the cut up side facing down.
3. Place the pan in the oven and let it cook for 38 to 44 min.
4. Once the time is up, allow the butternut squash to cool down completely. Peel it then chop it. Place a large pan over medium heat. Heat in it 1 tbsp of oil. Add the onion with beef meat and cook them for 12 min. Stir in the chopped butternut squash with cumin, Baharat, and sea salt. Mix them well.
5. Stir in the pine kernels and cook them for 2 min.
6. Stir in the water and bring them to a simmer. Put on the lid and let them cook for 9 to 11 min.
7. Get a small mixing bowl: Whisk in it the yogurt with garlic, a pinch of salt, lemon juice and 1 tbsp of olive oil.
8. Place dollops of the yogurt sauce over the beef skillet then serve it warm. Enjoy.

GOLDEN Chickpeas

Prep Time: 8 hrs
Total Time: 8 hrs 6 mins

Servings per Recipe: 4
Calories 178.5
Fat 1.7g
Cholesterol 0.0mg
Sodium 448.5mg
Carbohydrates 33.9g
Protein 7.4g

Ingredients

2 1/2 C. dry chickpeas, rinsed
olive oil
garlic salt
black pepper
clipped rosemary
soy sauce
oriental sesame oil
hot chili powder
tomato juice and curry powder

Directions

1. Get a large mixing bowl: Place in it the chickpeas and cover them with water. let them sit for an overnight.
2. Remove the chickpeas from the water and place them in a colander to dry for a bit.
3. For the pan:
4. Place a pan over medium heat. Heat in it a splash of oil. Toast in it the chickpeas with a pinch of salt and some herbs or spices of your choice.
5. For the oven:
6. Preheat the oven to 350 F.
7. Toss the chickpeas with some salt, herbs and spices of your choice. Spread it on a lined up cookie pan.
8. Place in it the oven and cook it for 15 min. Stir in it then let it cook for an extra 10 to 15 min.
9. Allow the roasted chickpeas to cool down completely then serve them as snack or topping.
10. Enjoy.

Lemon Wings

Prep Time: 1 hr 10 mins
Total Time: 1 hr 20 mins

Servings per Recipe: 4
Calories	532.9
Fat	41.5g
Cholesterol	150.9mg
Sodium	145.3mg
Carbohydrates	3.5g
Protein	36.4g

Ingredients

3 tbsp olive oil
1 lemon, juice
salt
black pepper
2 - 4 garlic cloves, crushed and minced
16 chicken wings
2 tbsp flat leaf parsley, chopped

Directions

1. Get a large mixing bowl: Whisk in it the olive oil with lemon juice, garlic, a pinch of salt and pepper.
2. Stir in the chicken wings and coat them with the mixture. Place the bowl in the fridge and let it sit for at least 60 min
3. Before you do anything else, preheat the grill and grease it.
4. Drain the chicken wings from the marinade and grill them for 5 to 7 min on each side.
5. Serve them with some yogurt and garnish them with some parsley.
6. Enjoy.

YOGURT and Chickpea Bake

Prep Time: 24 hrs
Total Time: 29 hrs

Servings per Recipe: 8
Calories 272.5
Fat 1.9g
Cholesterol 0.0mg
Sodium 614.9mg
Carbohydrates 53.3g
Protein 10.2g

Ingredients

2 1/4 lb. chickpeas
6 pita bread
3 C. plain Greek yogurt
2 tbsp ground cumin
2 garlic cloves, minced
salt
water
butter

Directions

1. Get a large mixing bowl: Place in it the chickpeas and cover them with water.
2. Let them sit for at least 10 h. Drain them and discard the water.
3. Place a large pot over medium high heat. Place in it the chickpeas and cover them with water.
4. Bring them to a rolling boil. Use a ladle to discard the foam the rise on top.
5. Lower the heat and let them cook for 4 h 20 min while adding more hot water if needed while.
6. Discard the white foam that rise on top every once in a while.
7. Before you do anything else, preheat the oven broiler to 500 F.
8. Split each pita bread into 2 halves to make two circles. Coat their open side with butter then cut each circle into 4 pieces.
9. Lay the pita pieces on a lined up baking sheet. Place the pan in the oven and let them cook for 4 to 5 min until they become golden and crunchy.
10. Get a mixing bowl: Mix in it the cumin, yogurt, garlic and 2 tsp salt.
11. Lay the pita chips in a casserole dish. Top it with 1 inch layer of the cooked chickpeas with some of their broth.
12. Pour over them the yogurt sauce then let the casserole sit for 12 min.
13. Garnish the chickpea casserole with some parsley then serve it.
14. Enjoy.

Sweet and Salty Lovers Skillet

Prep Time: 15 mins
Total Time: 50 mins

Servings per Recipe: 6
Calories	295.5
Fat	7.3g
Cholesterol	5.3mg
Sodium	297.8mg
Carbohydrates	51.0g
Protein	9.9g

Ingredients

- 2 tbsp olive oil
- 2 onions, chopped
- 10 garlic cloves, chopped
- 1 (14 oz.) cans diced tomatoes
- 4 carrots, sliced
- 2 medium potatoes, peeled and cubed
- 1/2 bunch parsley, cleaned and tied with string
- 1 tbsp brown sugar
- 1 1/2 tsp lemon pepper
- 1/2 tsp ground cinnamon
- 1/2 tsp ground coriander
- 2 medium zucchini, diced
- 1 (8 oz.) cans artichoke hearts, drained and quartered
- 1 (15 oz.) cans garbanzo beans, drained and rinsed
- 1 C. plain yogurt

Directions

1. Place a saucepan over medium heat. Heat in it the oil. Sauté in it the onion for 5 min.
2. Stir in the garlic and cook it for an extra minute. Stir in the tomatoes, carrots, potatoes and parsley.
3. Lower the heat and put on the lid. Let them cook for 22 min.
4. Once the time is up, stir in the brown sugar, lemon pepper, cinnamon, coriander, zucchini, artichoke hearts, and garbanzo beans.
5. Put on the lid and cook them for an extra 12 min. Drain the parsley and discard it.
6. Add the yogurt and stir it into the veggies stew. Garnish it with some nuts and serve it with some rice.
7. Enjoy.

LAMB ROLLS
Lebanese

Prep Time: 20 mins
Total Time: 1 hr 20 mins

Servings per Recipe: 10
Calories 250.6
Fat 12.8g
Cholesterol 33.1mg
Sodium 1333.8mg
Carbohydrates 24.6g
Protein 11.4g

Ingredients

1 (16 oz.) jars grape leaves
1 C. uncooked long grain rice
3 tbsp of mint
1 C. water
1 lb. ground lamb
2 tbsp pine nuts, toasted
2 tbsp dried currants
1/8 tsp cinnamon

1/4 allspice
1/2 tsp sugar
3 garlic cloves
2 - 3 lemons

Directions

1. Get a large bowl. Fill with hot water and 1 tablespoon of lemon juice.
2. Place in it the grape leaves and let them sit for 35 sec. Drain them and place them in a colander to cool down.
3. Lay some grape leaves in the bottom of a pot to cover it.
4. Get a mixing bowl: Mix in the meat with rice, mint, pinenuts, cinnamon, allspice, sugar, cloves, a pinch of salt and pepper to make the filling.
5. Lay a grape leaf on cutting board. Discard its stems. Lay 1 tsp of the filling on the bottom of it.
6. Pull the sides slightly the middle then roll the leaf over the filling. Place it in a the pot.
7. Repeat the process with the remaining leaves and filling.
8. Pour over them 1 C. of water with lemon juice. Put on the lid and cook them over high heat until they start boiling.
9. Lower the heat and let them cook for an extra 60 min.
10. Once the time is up, serve your stuffed grape leaves warm with some tomato sauce.
11. Enjoy.

Crunchy Beet Salad

🥣 Prep Time: 10 mins
🕐 Total Time: 1 hr 40 mins

Servings per Recipe: 4
Calories   74.5
Fat   4.6g
Cholesterol   0.0mg
Sodium   51.2mg
Carbohydrates   7.1g
Protein   1.3g

Ingredients

5 large beets
2 garlic cloves, crushed
2 tbsp cilantro, chopped
4 tbsp chives, chopped
4 tsp olive oil

4 tbsp vinegar
salt and pepper
4 tbsp parsley, chopped

Directions

1. Place a saucepan of water over medium heat. Cook in it the beets until they become soft.
2. Drain the beets and place them aside to cool down for a while.
3. Peel the beets and cut them into dices.
4. Get a mixing bowl: Toss in it the beet dices with garlic, cilantro, chives, olive oil, vinegar, salt and pepper.
5. Place the salad in the fridge for 60 min. Garnish it with some parsley then serve it.
6. Enjoy.

SPICY
Chicken Roast

Prep Time: 5 mins
Total Time: 50 mins

Servings per Recipe: 8
Calories 181.5
Fat 15.2g
Cholesterol 42.5mg
Sodium 39.8mg
Carbohydrates 0.0g
Protein 10.5g

Ingredients

1 chicken, cut into 8 pieces
1/4-1/2 C. olive oil
2 tbsp za'atar spice mix
salt

Directions

1. Get a small mixing bowl: Mix in it the oil with za'atar spice mix.
2. Season the chicken pieces of with some salt and pepper. Coat them with the oil and za'atar marinade.
3. Place the marinated chicken pieces in a zip lock bag and seal it. Place it in the fridge for 1 h to an overnight.
4. Before you do anything else, preheat the oven to 425 F.
5. Place the chicken pieces on a greased baking sheet. Place it in the oven and let them cook for 46 min.
6. Serve your roasted chicken warm with your favorite dip.
7. Enjoy.

Spring Veggies Salad with Tahini Sauce

Prep Time: 15 mins
Total Time: 15 mins

Servings per Recipe: 1
Calories   384.1
Fat   20.3g
Cholesterol   0.0mg
Sodium   689.2mg
Carbohydrates   48.1g
Protein   11.5g

Ingredients

- 3 - 4 C. raw kale, chopped
- 1/2-1 apple, chopped
- 1/4 C. raisins
- 1/4 C. toasted walnuts, coarsely chopped
- 1/4-1/2 C. carrot, grated
- 1/2 C. celery, chopped
- 1/2 C. edamame beans
- 1/4 C. mixed sprouts

TAHINI DRESSING
- 1/3 C. tahini
- 1/3 C. water
- 1/4 C. lemon juice
- 2 garlic cloves, minced
- 1/2-3/4 tsp sea salt
- 1 tsp honey

Directions

1. Get a serving bowl: Toss in it all the veggies and place it aside.
2. Combine the tahini with water, lemon juice, garlic, salt and honey in a food blender. Blend them smooth to make the dressing.
3. Drizzle the dressing over the salad and toss it to coat. Serve it right away.
4. Enjoy.

FRUITY Carrot Salad

Prep Time: 15 mins
Total Time: 15 mins

Servings per Recipe: 6
Calories 106.6
Fat 3.6g
Cholesterol 0.0mg
Sodium 30.9mg
Carbohydrates 19.1g
Protein 1.3g

Ingredients

2 C. shredded carrots
2 large oranges, peeled, sectioned, and cut into pieces
1/2 C. onion, sliced
1/3 C. raisins
1 1/2 tbsp vegetable oil

1 1/2 tbsp lemon juice
1 tbsp water

Directions

1. Get a mixing bowl: Toss in it the carrots with onion, raisins and oranges.
2. Get a small mixing bowl: Mix in it the water with lemon juice, and oil to make the dressing.
3. Drizzle the dressing over the salad. Place it in the fridge and let sit for at least 1 h
4. Toss the salad then serve it.
5. Enjoy.

Beef Kufta Casserole

Prep Time: 15 mins
Total Time: 1 hr

Servings per Recipe: 6
Calories	596.8
Fat	34.3g
Cholesterol	154.2mg
Sodium	164.4mg
Carbohydrates	24.6g
Protein	45.4g

Ingredients

3 lbs. ground beef
1 large onion, chopped
3/4-1 C. chopped parsley
4 garlic cloves, chopped
seasoning salt
allspice
black pepper
garlic powder

TOPPING
3 - 4 tomatoes, sliced
3 - 4 potatoes, sliced

Directions

1. Before you do anything, preheat the oven to 400 F. Grease a casserole dish.
2. Get a large mixing bowl: Mix in the onion, garlic, parsley, meat, some allspice, garlic powder, a pinch of salt and pepper.
3. Spoon the mixture into the baking dish. Spread it in an even layer.
4. Lay over it the potato slices followed by the tomato slices. Lay a sheet of foil over the casserole to cover it.
5. Place it in the oven and cook it for 46 min.
6. Enjoy.

ARABIAN
Tomato Sauce

🥣 Prep Time: 10 mins
🕐 Total Time: 20 mins

Servings per Recipe: 4
Calories 136.2
Fat 10.6g
Cholesterol 0.0mg
Sodium 13.4mg
Carbohydrates 10.0g
Protein 2.2g

Ingredients

2 C. shredded carrots
2 large oranges, peeled, sectioned, and cut into pieces
1/2 C. onion, sliced
1/3 C. raisins
1 1/2 tbsp vegetable oil

1 1/2 tbsp lemon juice
1 tbsp water

Directions

1. Get a large mixing bowl: Place in it the tomato and cover them with hot water.
2. Let them sit for few minutes. Drain the tomatoes and peel them. Discard the seeds and chop the flesh.
3. Place a pan over medium heat. Heat in it the oil. Cook in it the garlic with tomato for 6 min.
4. Stir in the mint with cayenne pepper, a pinch of salt and pepper. Cook them for an extra 6 min.
5. Serve your tomato sauce warm with some spaghetti or whatever you desire.
6. Enjoy.

Pomegranate Flowers Salad

Prep Time: 15 mins
Total Time: 40 mins

Servings per Recipe: 3
Calories   149.2
Fat   5.2g
Cholesterol   0.0mg
Sodium   60.7mg
Carbohydrates   24.0g
Protein   6.3g

Ingredients

1 head cauliflower
olive oil
sea salt
fresh ground black pepper
1/2 recipe tahini sauce
1/4 C. golden raisin

1/4 C. slivered almonds, toasted
1/4 C. pomegranate seeds

Directions

1. Before you do anything, preheat the oven to 410 F. Grease baking sheet.
2. Get a large mixing bowl: Toss in it the cauliflower florets with olive oil, a pinch of salt and pepper.
3. Spread them in the baking sheet.
4. Place the pan in the oven and cook it for 18 to 36 min or until they florets become golden brown.
5. Get a mixing bowl: Place in it the raisins and cover them with some hot water
6. Let them sit for few minutes until they become plump. Drain them and discard the water.
7. Get a serving bowl: Toss in it the roasted cauliflower with raisins, almonds, and tahini sauce.
8. Serve your salad right away or place it in the fridge until ready to serve.
9. Garnish it with the pomegranate seeds right before serving it.
10. Enjoy.

CLASSIC
Lebanese Chicken Kabobs

Prep Time: 4 hrs
Total Time: 4 hrs 20 mins

Servings per Recipe: 4
Calories 590.7
Fat 37.9 g
Cholesterol 163.9 mg
Sodium 175.6 mg
Carbohydrates 8.2 g
Protein 54.1 g

Ingredients

2 1/4 lb. chicken breast, cubed
10 garlic cloves, pressed
1 tsp ground cinnamon
1 tsp ground allspice
1 tsp cayenne pepper
1 tsp ground cardamom

1 lemon, juice
1/4 C. olive oil
1/2 C. plain yogurt
1/2 C. cilantro, chopped

Directions

1. Get a large mixing bowl: Whisk in it the garlic with cinnamon, allspice, cayenne pepper, cardamom, lemon juice, olive oil, yogurt and cilantro.
2. Add the chicken dices and toss them to coat with a pinch of salt and pepper.
3. Cover the bowl with a plastic wrap and let it sit for at least 5 h to marinate.
4. Before you do anything, preheat the oven to 400 F. Grease a casserole dish.
5. Thread the chicken dices into skewers. Grill them for 5 to 7 min on each side.
6. Serve your chicken kabobs warm with some pita bread and yogurt.
7. Enjoy.

Homemade Lebanese Chicken Burritos

Prep Time: 10 mins
Total Time: 25 mins

Servings per Recipe: 4
Calories   533.9
Fat   23.5g
Cholesterol   58.9mg
Sodium   717.0mg
Carbohydrates   53.0g
Protein   28.2g

Ingredients

3 boneless skinless chicken breasts, strips
2 tbsp olive oil
1 small onion, chopped
1 tbsp garlic, minced
1/4 C. lemon juice
1 tbsp cumin
1 tsp oregano
salt and pepper
4 burrito-size flour tortillas
FOR THE SAUCE
1/2 C. mayonnaise
3 tbsp lemon juice
3 tbsp garlic powder

TOPPINGS
1 tomatoes, chopped
1 small onion, chopped
1 C. lettuce, shredded
3 tbsp tahini sauce

Directions

1. Place a pan over medium heat. Heat in it the oil. Cook in it the chicken, chopped onion, minced garlic, 1/4 C. lemon juice, cumin, oregano and enough salt and pepper for 8 to 12 min.
2. Get a small mixing bowl: Whisk in it the mayo, lemon juice and garlic powder.
3. Place a large pan over medium heat. Heat in it the tortillas for 1 min on each side.
4. Lay a tortilla on a sheet of foil. lay over it 1/4 of the chicken, mayo dressing, tomato, onion, lettuce.
5. Wrap the tortilla over the filling like a burrito style. Place it aside.
6. Repeat the process with the remaining ingredients. Serve your burritos right away with your favorite dipping sauce. Enjoy.

MINTY
Warm Mushroom Salad

Prep Time: 5 mins
Total Time: 20 mins

Servings per Recipe: 4
Calories 113.2
Fat 10.5g
Cholesterol 0.0mg
Sodium 5.7mg
Carbohydrates 3.9g
Protein 2.8g

Ingredients

12 oz. whole mushrooms, sliced
1/2 tsp ground cinnamon
1 pinch ground cloves
1 1/2 tsp ground coriander
3 tbsp olive oil
1 1/2 tbsp lemon juice

1 tbsp chopped parsley
2 tsp chopped mint
salt
black pepper

Directions

1. Place a pan over medium heat. Heat in it the oil. Cook in it the mushrooms, cinnamon, cloves and coriander for 5 to 7 min.
2. Stir in the lemon juice with parsley, mint, a pinch of salt and pepper.
3. Serve your salad warm with your favorite toppings.
4. Enjoy.

Pistachios Baklava with Honey and Pomegranate Syrup

Prep Time: 1 hr
Total Time: 2 hrs

Servings per Recipe: 24
Calories   318.6
Fat   18.5g
Cholesterol   20.3mg
Sodium   176.9mg
Carbohydrates   36.2g
Protein   5.2g

Ingredients

SYRUP
1 C. sugar
1/4 C. water
1/4 C. pomegranate syrup
1/4 C. orange juice
1 orange, zest of
1 cinnamon stick
1 C. honey
1/4 C. water

PASTRY
1 (16 oz.) packages phyllo dough, thawed
1 C. butter

FILLING
10 oz. roasted & salted pistachios
2 oz. pecans
4 oz. almonds
2 tsp cinnamon
1 tbsp sugar
1 dash ground cloves
1/2 tsp cayenne pepper

Directions

1. To make the syrup:
2. Place a heavy saucepan over medium high heat. Stir in it the sugar, 1/4 C. of Water, Pomegranate syrup, orange juice, zest, and cinnamon stick.
3. Cook them while stirring them all the time until the sugar dissolves and the mixture starts to boil.
4. Stir in the honey and lower the heat. Let the syrup cook for an extra 15 min until it starts bubbling.
5. Turn off the heat. Use a tsp to drop some of the syrup on the kitchen counter.
6. If the syrup became hard, add to it some water and mix it well. If it stays liquid then it is done. Place it aside to cool down.
7. To make the baklava:
8. Get a mixing bowl: Mix in it all the filling ingredients.

9. Before you do anything else, preheat the oven to 400 F. Greased a baking dish with some butter.
10. Place 10 phyllo sheets in the bottom of the greased dish while brushing each one of them with melted butter.
11. Spread over them 1/3 of the filling.
12. Cover them with 6 phyllo sheets while brushing each one of them with melted butter before adding another.
13. Repeat the process to another 2 layers, ending with 8 phyllo sheets on top.
14. Use a sharp knife or a pizza cutter to cut the baklava into diamonds shape. Place it in the oven and bake it for 16 min.
15. Lower the oven heat to 300 F. Bake it for an extra 42 min until they become golden brown.
16. Once the time is up, place the hot baklava pan on the kitchen counter.
17. Pour the cold syrup all over it and let it sit for at least 10 min.
18. Serve your baklava diamonds right away or store them in an airtight container.
19. Serve it with some mint tea.
20. Enjoy.

Trick or Treat
Date Cookies

🍲 Prep Time: 15 mins
🕐 Total Time: 40 mins

Servings per Recipe: 1
Calories	1435.5
Fat	50.7g
Cholesterol	227.8mg
Sodium	336.8mg
Carbohydrates	221.1g
Protein	27.9g

Ingredients

- 1/2 tsp active dry yeast
- 1/4 C. lukewarm water
- 1 tbsp orange flower water
- 1 large egg
- 8 tbsp unsalted butter, melted and cooled
- 1 1/2 C. coarse semolina
- 2 tbsp sugar
- 1/4 tsp salt
- 1 C. all-purpose flour
- milk
- FILLING
- 3/4 C. honey dates
- 3 tbsp sugar
- 1 1/2 tsp orange flower water
- 1 1/2 tsp rose water

Directions

1. To make the dough:
2. Get a large mixing bowl: Stir in the yeast with water. Let them sit for 8 min.
3. Add the flower water, egg, and melted butter. Mix them well.
4. Stir in the semolina followed by sugar and a pinch of salt. add the flour and mix them well. Cover the bowl with a food plastic wrap. Let it sit for 60 min.
5. Before you do anything, preheat the oven to 400 F. Line up 2 baking sheets with parchment paper.
6. To make the filling:
7. Get a food blender: Blend in it all the filling ingredients until they become smooth.
8. Place 1 tbsp of dough in the palm of your hand. Flatten it into a 3 inches circle with your hand. Place in the middle of it 1 1/2 tsp of the filling. Pull the dough over the filling to cover it. Place it with the seam facing down on a lined up baking sheet. Repeat the process with the remaining dough and filling.
9. Place the cookie sheets in the oven and bake them for 22 to 24 min.
10. Allow the cookies to cool down completely then serve them with some tea. Enjoy.

SAUCY
Okra Burger Pan

Prep Time: 10 mins
Total Time: 55 mins

Servings per Recipe: 4
Calories 382.0
Fat 23.5g
Cholesterol 76.1mg
Sodium 92.8mg
Carbohydrates 17.2g
Protein 27.3g

Ingredients

1 lb. okra, small, top removed
1 lb. hamburger
4 tomatoes, chopped
1 onion, chopped
1 tsp allspice, ground
1/2 tsp cinnamon, ground

TOPPING
3 tbsp olive oil
5 garlic cloves, sliced

Directions

1. Before you do anything, preheat the oven to 400 F. Grease a casserole dish.
2. Get a large mixing bowl: Combine in it the okra, hamburger, tomatoes, onion, allspice, and cinnamon.
3. Pour the mixture in the greased dish and spread it into an even layer.
4. Place the casserole in the oven and let it cook for 46 min.
5. In the meantime, Place small skillet over medium heat. Heat in it the oil.
6. Add the garlic and cook it until it becomes golden and crisp. Turn off the heat.
7. When the okra burger casserole is done, drizzle over it the garlic and oil mix. Serve it warm with some rice.
8. Enjoy.

Tahini Meatloaf

Prep Time: 2 hrs
Total Time: 2 hrs 30 mins

Servings per Recipe: 4
Calories   691.7
Fat   38.1g
Cholesterol   82.5mg
Sodium   390.9mg
Carbohydrates   55.5g
Protein   30.4g

Ingredients

Dough
3/4 C. water
1 tsp honey
2 tsp yeast
3 tbsp olive oil
2 C. flour
1/2 tsp salt
Filling
1 lb. ground beef
1 onion, chopped
2 tbsp olive oil
1/2 tsp allspice
1/4 tsp cardamom
1/4 tsp cinnamon
1 tbsp tahini
1 tbsp sour cream
1 tbsp pomegranate molasses
Toppings
1 tbsp water
2 tbsp powdered milk

Directions

1. To make the dough:
2. Get a large mixing bowl: Stir in the water with honey and yeast. Let them sit for 8 min.
3. Mix in the oil with flour and salt. Combine them until your get a soft dough.
4. Place the dough on a floured surface and knead it for 2 to 3 min until it becomes soft.
5. Place the dough in a greased bowl and cover it with kitchen towel. Let rest until it doubles in size.
6. To make the Filling:
7. Place a pan over medium heat. Heat in it the oil. Cook in it the onion with beef, allspice, cardamom, and cinnamon for 8 min.
8. Stir in the tahini, sour cream, and pomegranate molasses. Season them with a pinch of salt and pepper.
9. Turn off the heat and allow the filling to cool down completely.

10. Before you do anything, preheat the oven to 450 F. Coat a cookie sheet with a cooking spray.
11. Divide the dough into 4 portions. Roll a ball of dough into a circle.
12. Place in the middle of it 1/4 of the filling. Pull the edges on top of the filling.
13. Twist them and press them to seal them. Place stuffed dough on the cookie sheet with the seam facing down.
14. Repeat the process with the remaining dough and filling. Cover the meatloaves with a wet towel and let them rest for 11 min.
15. Get a mixing bowl: Whisk in it the water with powdered milk. Coat the stuffed loaves with it.
16. Place the meatloaves in the oven and let them cook for 10 to 12 min until they become golden brown.
17. Serve your meatloaves warm with some ketchup.
18. Enjoy.

Neon Pilaf

Prep Time: 5 mins
Total Time: 25 mins

Servings per Recipe: 6
Calories   156.0
Fat   1.8g
Cholesterol   0.0mg
Sodium   399.1mg
Carbohydrates   31.0g
Protein   3.2g

Ingredients

- 1 C. rice
- 1/2 red pepper, diced
- 1 small onion, chopped
- 1 diced carrot
- 1 crushed garlic clove
- 1/2 C. peas
- 2 tsp oil
- 1 bay leaf
- 1 tsp grated ginger
- 1 tsp salt
- 1 tbsp chopped parsley
- 2 C. water
- 1 pinch pepper
- 1/2 tsp turmeric
- 1 tsp butter

Directions

1. Place a pot over medium heat. Heat in it the oil. Cook in it the onions, carrots, peppers, and peas for 4 min.
2. Stir in the garlic with ginger, bay leaf, pepper, and turmeric. Cook them for 6 min over low heat.
3. Stir in the broth with a pinch of salt. Put on the lid and cook them until they start boiling.
4. Once the time is up, stir in the bring and bring them to another boil. Put on the lid and let the pilaf coo for 16 to 21 min over low heat.
5. Use a fork to fluff the pilaf then serve it warm or cold.
6. Enjoy.

FRIED MEATY
Eggplant Stew

🥣 Prep Time: 1 hr
🕒 Total Time: 2 hrs

Servings per Recipe: 6
Calories   149.8
Fat   6.2g
Cholesterol   25.7mg
Sodium   506.4mg
Carbohydrates   16.0g
Protein   9.9g

Ingredients

2 eggplants, peeled and diced
1/2 lb. ground beef
1 onion, chopped
1 tsp salt
1/2 tsp pepper
1 tsp allspice
1/2 tsp cinnamon
1 (16 oz.) cans chopped tomatoes
4 tbsp tomato paste
2 C. water
oil

Directions

1. Place the eggplant dices in a colander. Season them with 1 tsp of salt. Let them sit for 12 to 30 min.
2. Pat the eggplant dices dry.
3. Place a pan over medium heat. Heat in it the oil. Cook in it the eggplant dices until they become golden and soft.
4. Drain them and place them aside.
5. Place a pot over medium heat. Cook in it the beef for 5 min. Stir in the onion and cook them for another 5 min.
6. Stir in the spices and cook them for an extra min.
7. Stir in the cooked eggplant with tomato paste, tomatoes and water.
8. Put on the lid and let them cook for 35 min to 55 min until the meat and eggplant are done.
9. Serve your eggplant stew warm with some rice.
10. Enjoy.

Ricy Meatballs Soup

Prep Time: 10 mins
Total Time: 35 mins

Servings per Recipe: 6
Calories   257.9
Fat   13.9g
Cholesterol   41.9mg
Sodium   619.9mg
Carbohydrates   21.4g
Protein   10.6g

Ingredients

- 10.5 oz. ground lamb, prepared for kafta
- 5 oz. long grain rice, rinsed and drained
- 4 tbsp tomato puree
- 1 tbsp instant chicken bouillon granules
- 8 1/2 C. water
- 1 tbsp clarified butter

Directions

1. Shape the lamb kafta into bite size meatballs
2. Place a large saucepan over medium heat. Heat in it the oil. Cook in it the meatballs for 3 to 4 min.
3. Stir in the tomato purée and cook them until they start boiling.
4. Stir in the rice, chicken stock granules and the water. Let them cook over low heat until the rice is done.
5. Serve your soup warm.
6. Enjoy.

CREAMY SERRANO and Cucumber Salad

Prep Time: 5 mins
Total Time: 5 mins

Servings per Recipe: 2
Calories   70.8
Fat   2.7g
Cholesterol   10.6mg
Sodium   622.2mg
Carbohydrates   9.6g
Protein   3.5g

Ingredients

1/2 English cucumber, diced
1/4 C. lemon juice
2/3 C. middle eastern style yogurt
1/4 C. water
1/2-1 small garlic clove, minced
1/2-1 whole serrano pepper, minced

1/2 tsp salt
3/4 tsp dried mint
olive oil

Directions

1. Get a large mixing bowl: Whisk in it the garlic, lemon juice, yogurt, water, serrano pepper, salt and mint.
2. Stir the diced cucumber into the yogurt sauce. Pour the mixture into in a serving bowl.
3. Place the salad in the fridge until ready to serve.
4. Drizzle some olive oil over the salad before serving it.
5. Enjoy.

Lebanese Style Chicken Couscous

Prep Time: 20 mins
Total Time: 2 hrs 20 mins

Servings per Recipe: 6
Calories   655.3
Fat   33.0g
Cholesterol   130.9mg
Sodium   147.5mg
Carbohydrates   49.1g
Protein   37.8g

Ingredients

- 2 tbsp olive oil
- 1 large onion
- 4 garlic cloves, crushed
- 3 1/2 lbs. chicken
- 1/2 tsp ginger
- 2 tsp cinnamon
- 1 tsp cardamom
- 1/2 tsp cumin
- 1/2 tsp Aleppo pepper
- salt and pepper
- 1 1/2 tbsp lemon juice
- 2 C. couscous, Lebanese-style
- 2 tbsp butter

Directions

1. Place a pan over medium heat. Heat in it the oil. Cook in it the garlic with onion for 3 min.
2. Stir in it the chicken with 4 1/2 C. of water, cinnamon, ginger, cardamom, cumin, Aleppo pepper, a pinch of salt and pepper.
3. Put on the lid and let the chicken stew cook for 1 h 30 min until the chicken is done.
4. Once the time is up, drain the chicken pieces and shred them. Discard the bones.
5. Cook the remaining sauce in the pan until it starts boiling. Stir into it the lemon juice followed by the couscous.
6. Let it cook for 9 min while stirring it often. Add the butter and stir them well.
7. Place the chicken pieces on top and put on the lid. Turn off the heat and let the couscous rest for 2 to 3 min.
8. Serve your couscous skillet warm.
9. Enjoy.

TRIPOLI
Lamb Gyros

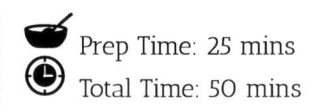

Prep Time: 25 mins
Total Time: 50 mins

Servings per Recipe: 4
Calories 434.9
Fat 28.6g
Cholesterol 129.4mg
Sodium 192.7mg
Carbohydrates 20.6g
Protein 23.4g

Ingredients

1 lb. ground lamb
1/4 C. golden raisin, chopped
1/4 tsp ground cinnamon
kosher salt and pepper
1/2 C. breadcrumbs
1 large egg, beaten

1 bunch scallion, sliced
4 pieces flat bread
1/2 C. Greek yogurt
2 tbsp of mint

Directions

1. Before you do anything, preheat the oven broiler.
2. Get a large mixing bowl: Mix in it the lamb, raisins, cinnamon, 1 1/2 tsp salt, 1/4 tsp pepper, the bread crumbs, egg, and 3/4 of the scallions.
3. Shape the mixture into medium size meatballs. Lay them on a foil lined up baking sheet.
4. Place the meatballs sheet in the oven and cook them for 7 to 8 min.
5. Place the bread on serving plates. Lay over it the meatballs followed by the yogurt, mint and scallions.
6. Add your favorite toppings like tomato and lettuce. Serve your gyros right away.
7. Enjoy.

Beirut Bread

🥣 Prep Time: 25 mins
🕐 Total Time: 1 hr 15 mins

Servings per Recipe: 36
Calories   64.0
Fat   4.0g
Cholesterol   4.6mg
Sodium   175.2mg
Carbohydrates   6.2g
Protein   0.9g

Ingredients

- 8.8 flour
- 1 1/2 tsp baking powder
- 1/2 tsp salt
- 1/4 C. light fruity olive oil
- 1/4 C. orange juice
- 7 oz. pitted green olives, chopped
- 7 oz. pitted black olives, chopped
- 1/4 tsp cayenne pepper
- 1 tbsp chopped oregano
- 1 egg yolk, lightly beaten
- 2 tsp milk

Directions

1. To make the dough:
2. Get a large mixing bowl: Mix in it the flour with baking powder, oil, orange juice and a pinch of salt until you get a dough.
3. Shape the dough into a ball and place it in a greased bowl. Cover it with a towel and let it sit for 35 min.
4. Before you do anything, preheat the oven to 356 F. Grease a baking sheet.
5. To make the filling:
6. Get a mixing bowl: Mix in it the olives with cayenne pepper, oregano, a pinch of salt and pepper. Place half of dough on a floured board. Roll it into 8/9 inches rectangle. Spread over it half of the olives filling.
7. Roll the rectangle over the filling into a log. Place it on the greased baking sheet.
8. Repeat the process with the other half of the dough and filling.
9. Get a small mixing bowl: Whisk in it the egg yolk with milk. Coat the bread loaves with it.
10. Place the bread loaves in the oven and bake them for 36 to 42 min until they become golden brown.
11. Allow the olive loaves to cool down completely then serve them your favorite dipping sauce.Enjoy.

MINTY
Potato Salad

Prep Time: 20 mins
Total Time: 50 mins

Servings per Recipe: 8
Calories   137.7
Fat   5.2g
Cholesterol   0.0mg
Sodium   154.3mg
Carbohydrates   21.2g
Protein   2.5g

Ingredients

2 lbs. russet potatoes
1/4 C. lemon juice
3 tbsp extra-virgin olive oil
1/2 tsp salt
ground pepper
4 scallions, sliced

1/4 C. chopped of mint

Directions

1. Place a large pan of water over medium high heat. Stir in it a pinch of salt then heat it until it starts boiling.
2. Add to it the potatoes and cook them for 20 to 30 min until they become soft.
3. Remove the potatoes from the water and run them under some cool water. Place them aside to cool down.
4. Slice the potatoes into small dices.
5. Get a serving bowl: Mix in it the lemon juice, oil, salt and pepper. Stir in the potato.
6. Place the salad in the fridge until ready to serve.
7. Stir into it the mint and scallions right before serving it.
8. Enjoy.

Hot Pepper Hummus Dip

Prep Time: 10 mins
Total Time: 1 hr 5 mins

Servings per Recipe: 24
Calories   699.6
Fat   42.1g
Cholesterol   0.0mg
Sodium   1206.2mg
Carbohydrates   67.3g
Protein   21.5g

Ingredients

- 3 red bell peppers
- 3 C. chickpeas, cooked and rinsed
- 1 tbsp garlic, minced
- 1 C. tahini
- 1/2 C. lemon juice
- 1 tbsp paprika
- 1 tbsp chili powder
- 2 tsp cumin, ground
- 1 tsp salt
- 1/2 tsp cayenne pepper
- 3 tbsp virgin olive oil
- 1/4 C. parsley, minced

Directions

1. Before you do anything, preheat the oven to 400 F. Grease a casserole dish.
2. Place the peppers with their cut up side facing down on a lined up baking sheet.
3. Cook them for 12 min until their skin become black. Place them in a zip lock bag and close it. Let them sit for 16 min.
4. Discard the black skin from the peppers.
5. Place them in a blender with garlic and chickpeas. Blend them smooth.
6. Mix in the tahini, lemon, paprika, chili powder, cumin, salt and cayenne pepper.
7. Serve your pepper spread with some pita bread, bread sticks, pierogis or stuffed bread.
8. Enjoy.

SAUCY Lamb Stuffed Zucchini

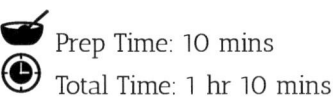

Prep Time: 10 mins
Total Time: 1 hr 10 mins

Servings per Recipe: 4
Calories 426.6
Fat 21.9g
Cholesterol 62.2mg
Sodium 1278.6mg
Carbohydrates 38.2g
Protein 23.0g

Ingredients

8 zucchini, ends trimmed
12 oz. ground lamb
3/4 C. instant brown rice
1 3/4 tsp dried marjoram, divided
1 1/4 tsp ground cumin, divided
1 1/4 tsp dried mint, divided
1/4 tsp ground allspice, divided
1/4 tsp salt
1 pinch cayenne pepper
1 (28 oz.) cans tomato sauce

Directions

1. Before you do anything, preheat the oven to 350 F. Get a casserole dish.
2. Use a coring knife to remove the pulp of the zucchini and leave them hollow.
3. Get a large mixing bowl: Mix in it the lamb, rice, 1 1/4 tsp marjoram, 3/4 tsp cumin, 1/2 tsp mint, 1/8 tsp allspice, salt and cayenne.
4. Spoon the minute into the zucchinis to stuff them. Place them in the casserole dish.
5. Place a large saucepan over medium heat. Stir in it the tomato sauce with the remaining 1/2 tsp marjoram, 1/2 tsp cumin, 3/4 tsp mint and 1/8 tsp allspice.
6. Cook them until they start boiling. Spread it over the stuffed zucchinis.
7. Place a sheet of foil over the zucchini casserole to cover it. Place it in the oven and let it cook for 22 min.
8. Turn over the zucchinis and cook them for an extra 22 min.
9. Serve your stuffed zucchinis warm with some rice.
10. Enjoy.

Homemade Tahini Hummus

Prep Time: 24 hrs
Total Time: 25 hrs

Servings per Recipe: 6
Calories	200.3
Fat	15.4g
Cholesterol	0.0mg
Sodium	131.6mg
Carbohydrates	13.6g
Protein	3.6g

Ingredients

8 oz. chickpeas, soaked water overnight
2 lemons, juice of
3 tbsp tahini
3 garlic cloves, crushed
salt
4 tbsp olive oil

GARNISH WITH
1 tbsp olive oil
1 tsp paprika
1 tsp ground cumin
2 sprigs parsley, chopped

Directions

1. Place a large saucepan of water over medium heat. Place in it the chickpeas and cover them with water.
2. Bring them to a boil. Lower the heat and let them cook for 60 min until the chickpeas become soft.
3. Drain the chickpeas and place the cooking water aside.
4. Get a food processor: Place in it the chickpeas with lemon juice, tahina, garlic, olive oil, salt.
5. Pulse them several times until they become smooth while adding the chickpea water if the mix is too thick.
6. Serve your hummus with some bread, veggies or toss it with some rice.
7. Enjoy.

TROPICAL
Coconut Cookies

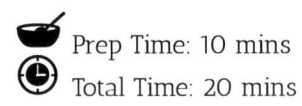

Prep Time: 10 mins
Total Time: 20 mins

Servings per Recipe: 30
Calories   69.3
Fat   3.6g
Cholesterol   4.0mg
Sodium   40.3mg
Carbohydrates   8.5g
Protein   0.8g

Ingredients

1/4 C. butter
1/4 C. vegetable shortening
1/8 C. shredded coconut, toasted
1 C. quick-cooking oatmeal, uncooked
1/2 C. granulated sugar
1 C. all-purpose flour

1/2 tsp baking powder
1/4 tsp salt
1/4 C. room temperature water
1 tsp vanilla

Directions

1. Before you do anything, preheat the oven to 400 F. Line up a baking sheet with a parchment paper.
2. Get a large mixing bowl: Mix in it all the ingredients until your get smooth dough.
3. Shape the cookie dough into bite size balls. Place in it the cookie balls.
4. Place the cookie pan in the oven and cook them for 11 min until they become golden brown
5. Allow the cookies to cool down completely then serve them.
6. Enjoy.

Cream Stuffed Potato Boats

🥣 Prep Time: 20 mins
🕐 Total Time: 1 hr 50 mins

Servings per Recipe: 4
Calories	327.6
Fat	7.3g
Cholesterol	2.4mg
Sodium	359.9mg
Carbohydrates	56.3g
Protein	10.8g

Ingredients

- 4 baking potatoes, rinsed and dried
- 1 tbsp olive oil
- 1 (430 g) cans chickpeas, drained
- 1 tsp coriander
- 1 tsp ground cumin
- 4 tbsp coriander, chopped
- 2 garlic cloves, crushed
- 2/3 C. natural low-fat yogurt
- 1 tbsp tahini
- salt & ground black pepper

Directions

1. Before you do anything, preheat the oven to 400 F.
2. Use a fork to prick the potatoes all over. Coat them with olive oil then place them on a lined up baking sheet.
3. Season them with some salt and pepper. Place the potato pan in the oven and cook them for 20 to 35 min until they become tender.
4. Once the time is up, place the baked potatoes aside to cool down for several minutes.
5. Get a large mixing bowl: Mash in it the chickpeas slightly. Mix in the ground coriander, the cumin, the crushed garlic and half the fresh coriander.
6. Gently slice the potatoes in half leaving the shell intact.
7. Gently scoop out some of the potato flesh but not all of it, leaving it empty in the middle.
8. Use a potato masher or a fork to mash the potato flesh. Add it to the chickpea mixture and combine them well to make the filling.
9. Adjust the seasoning of the filling. Spoon it into the potato shells and place them back on the baking sheet.
10. Place the pan in the oven and cook them for 12 to 16 min.
11. Garnish your potato boats with some coriander and yogurt or sour cream then serve them. Enjoy.

CREAMY Herbed Lentils Salad

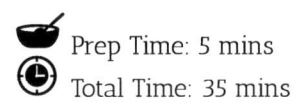

Prep Time: 5 mins
Total Time: 35 mins

Servings per Recipe: 8
Calories   120.9
Fat   0.3g
Cholesterol   1.2mg
Sodium   52.6mg
Carbohydrates   19.5g
Protein   9.7g

Ingredients

- 1 C. dry lentils, rinsed
- 6 C. water
- 2 C. non-fat yogurt
- 1/4 C. fresh cilantro, chopped
- 2 garlic cloves, minced
- 1 tsp dried thyme
- 1 pinch cayenne
- salt and pepper

Directions

1. Place a saucepan over medium heat. Stir in it the lentils with water and a pinch of salt
2. Cook them until they start boiling. Put on the lid and lower the heat. Cook the lentils until they become soft for 24 to 28 min.
3. Pour the lentils in a fine mesh sieve to drain them.
4. Get a mixing bowl: Toss in it the lentils with yogurt, cilantro, thyme, garlic, cayenne pepper, a pinch of salt and pepper.
5. Serve your salad right away.
6. Enjoy.

Classic Dark Baba Ganouj

Prep Time: 30 mins
Total Time: 1 hr

Servings per Recipe: 1
Calories	140.1
Fat	7.5g
Cholesterol	0.0mg
Sodium	15.5mg
Carbohydrates	17.7g
Protein	4.7g

Ingredients

- 2 medium dark-skinned eggplants
- 4 -5 garlic cloves
- 6 tbsp tahini
- 4 lemons, juice of
- 2 tbsp water
- salt & ground black pepper
- 1 dash hot red pepper
- chopped parsley
- toasted pine nuts
- pomegranate seeds

Directions

1. Before you do anything, preheat the oven to 400 F.
2. Place the eggplants on foil lined up baking sheet. Broil them for 20 to 30 min.
3. Allow the eggplants to cool down for a while. Peel them and mash them.
4. Get a food blender: Combine in it the garlic with tahini, lemon juice, and water until they become smooth.
5. Mix in the mashed eggplant until they become smooth.
6. Adjust the seasoning of the baba ganouj spread. Place it in the fridge for at least 60 min.
7. Serve your baba ganouj spread with some bread, rice or veggies.
8. Enjoy.

LOULOU'S Za'atar

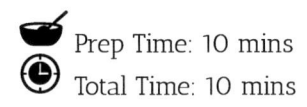

Prep Time: 10 mins
Total Time: 10 mins

Servings per Recipe: 1
Calories   261.2
Fat   14.6g
Cholesterol   0.0mg
Sodium   1563.8mg
Carbohydrates   36.8g
Protein   7.3g

Ingredients

1/2 C. savory or thyme
1/4 C. sumac
1/2 tsp sea salt

2 tbsps sesame seeds

Directions

1. Add the following to a mortar and pestle: sesame seeds, savory, salt, and sumac. Work the mix into a smooth powder.
2. Pour everything into a storage container, and keep it in the cupboard.
3. Enjoy.

Za'atar II

Prep Time: 5 mins
Total Time: 5 mins

Servings per Recipe: 1
Calories   367.8
Fat   28.3g
Cholesterol   0.0mg
Sodium   18621.4mg
Carbohydrates   25.4g
Protein   11.7g

Ingredients

- 4 tbsps ground sumac
- 2 tbsps whole thyme
- 3 tbsps toasted sesame seeds
- 2 tbsps oregano
- 2 tbsps ground marjoram
- 1 tsp savory
- 1 tsp basil
- 2 tbsps kosher salt

Directions

1. Get a food processor or blender and add the following to it: sumac, thyme, sesame seeds, oregano, marjoram, savory, basil, and salt.
2. Pulse the mix for a few mins until everything is smooth.
3. Add the mix to a storage container.
4. Enjoy.

ALTERNATIVE Za'atar (No Sumac)

Prep Time: 10 mins
Total Time: 10 mins

Servings per Recipe: 1
Calories	746.0
Fat	61.7g
Cholesterol	0.0mg
Sodium	5251.4mg
Carbohydrates	39.1g
Protein	22.8g

Ingredients

3 tbsps toasted sesame seeds
2 tbsps thyme
1 tbsp marjoram
1/2-1 tbsp finely grated lemon zest
1 tsp kosher salt

Directions

1. Place your toasted sesame seeds into a blender. Work the mix into a smooth powder.
2. Get a bowl, and add in your: powdered sesame seeds, thyme, marjoram, lemon zest, and salt.
3. Stir the mix completely, then pour everything into storage containers.
4. Enjoy.

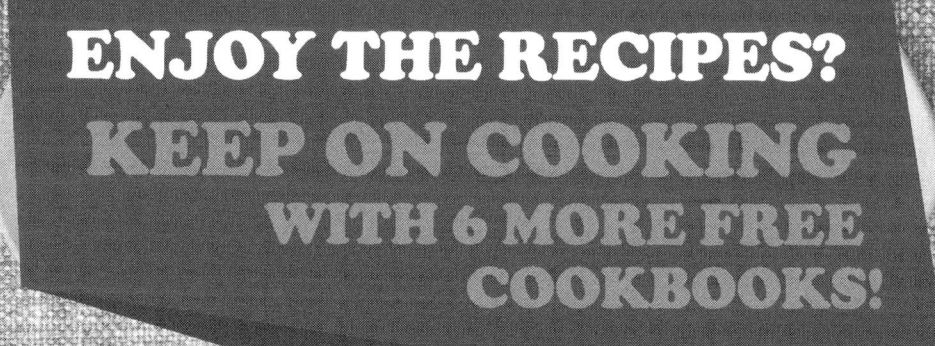

ENJOY THE RECIPES?
KEEP ON COOKING WITH 6 MORE FREE COOKBOOKS!

Visit our website and simply enter your email address to join the club and receive your 6 cookbooks.

http://booksumo.com/magnet

https://www.instagram.com/booksumopress/

https://www.facebook.com/booksumo/

Printed in Great Britain
by Amazon